Bread of Life

lenten reflections

for individuals

and groups

BARBARA J. ESSEX

UNITED CHURCH PRESS
Cleveland, Ohio

United Church Press, Cleveland, Ohio 44115
© 1998 by United Church Press

Printed in the United States of America on acid-free paper

03 02 01 00 99 98   5 4 3 2 1

Library of Congress Cataloging-in-Publication Data

Essex, Barbara J. (Barbara Jean), 1951–
    Bread of life : Lenten reflections for individuals and groups /
    Barbara J. Essex.
        p.   cm.
    Includes bibliographical references.
    ISBN 0-8298-1276-8 (paper : alk. paper)
    1. Lent—Meditations.   2. Bible. N.T. John—Study and teaching.
    3. Jesus Christ—Words—Study and teaching.   I. Title.
    BV85.E77   1998
    242'.34—dc21   98-36244
                                                              CIP

To the memories of my grandmothers:

Corine Simmons Avery,
who taught me to love God,
and
Pandora Essex Fluker,
who taught me to love the Bible

CONTENTS

GETTING STARTED

THIS LENTEN REFLECTION AND BIBLE STUDY resource is designed for use by individuals or by small groups. It consists of an introduction, seven Bible studies, and a short bibliography for further study. It is suggested that you plan for an eight-week period of study, with the first session covering the information in the introduction. If this resource is to be used in a small group, use the first session for community-building. Each subsequent week should be devoted to one Bible study. Each session is designed to last a minimum of ninety minutes. Individuals should keep a journal to record their reflections and questions. Always begin and end each session with prayer.

INTRODUCTION

Community-Building
Begin with prayer

OVERVIEW

"I LOVE GOD!" What a marvelous declaration. It is filled with hope and expectation. It is a confession of faith developed through the joys and sorrows of living. It is a proclamation grounded in and centered on a personal relationship with Jesus Christ. But can we love someone we do not truly know? And how can we *know* Jesus when other things are clamoring for our attention and our allegiance: television, busyness, work, family demands, and church obligations? How can we know the path to Jesus when other paths, including New Age spirituality, beckon? Further, what do we gain by believing in and following Jesus? Do we simply become "better" people? Are we moved to some thing or some place beyond our personal relationship with Christ? Faith is personal, but it is not private. Faith that does not reach outward is hardly faith.

I take special joy in sharing with you the excitement of my relationship with Christ. Lent is the ideal time to explore Jesus' journey from death to resurrection. This is an opportunity for us to be challenged, inspired, and informed as we seek a deeper faith and closer communion with one another.

Lent is the forty-day devotional period before Easter. It is a time when Christians across the world take time out to reflect on and to prepare for the work of ministry and service to God and to all of creation. It is a time to exercise the disciplines of mind, body, and spirit through prayer, study, fasting, and worship. *Bread of Life* is intended to assist you in reflecting on selected passages from the Gospel of John, specifically the "I am" sayings of Jesus. The themes that these passages highlight are those often encountered on the pilgrimage of life and faith. Discussion of biblical texts provides opportunities to reflect on lenten themes and to reflect on the issues of our day.

This book is designed for ministers and laypersons who want to journey with Jesus. The Gospel of John is my favorite book in the New Testament! But, I warn you—the going will not be easy. This version of the life, ministry, death, and resurrection of Jesus is moving, poignant, life-changing, and life-giving. There are words that push and prod as well as words that comfort and console. This Gospel is high drama, yet it is a difficult book to grasp. The language is poetic, but there are long speeches and convoluted debates. There are confusing timelines and repeated phrases. It takes real commitment to read and understand John's Gospel, but the struggle is worth it!

Bread of Life will neither answer all your questions about John's Gospel nor provide the many details needed to fully unravel its meanings. This volume will not summarize the tomes of scholarly and technical commentary written about this Gospel. So, what, you may be asking, *will* this volume do? I hope it will serve as a springboard for ongoing, in-depth study. I hope it will compel you to think about your faith and to share your reflections with others. I hope it will bring you closer to God, knowing that this is a relationship worth developing and nurturing. I hope it will bring you to Easter experiencing the cost and the joy of discipleship.

The Gospel of John has generated a great deal of scholarly attention, yet it is intermittently used in the lectionary and is often misunderstood. There are many unanswered questions concerning this book. For example, scholars are divided over its authorship. Although this Gospel has long been considered the work of the apostle John, the son of Zebedee, who was one of Jesus' twelve disciples, scholars are not convinced that the apostle is the author. Within the Gospel itself, the writer is identified as the "beloved disciple" (see John 13:23 and 21:24), an unnamed follower of Jesus who plays an important role in the book. Tradition has identified the beloved disciple with John, the son of Zebedee, but it cannot be proven from the Gospel itself. We can only say that John's Gospel was produced by a Jewish believer in Jesus, one of a group of like-minded folk who had broken with the synagogue. The authorship of the book remains unsettled.

The Gospel of John is "asynoptic." It is different from the "Synoptic" (literally, "seen together") Gospels—Matthew, Mark, and Luke. The Synoptics provide similar portrayals of Jesus and share much of the same material. They are similar in outline, content, chronology, and wording. John's Gospel, on the other hand, is a peculiar book that is filled with different images and concepts. John's Gospel is a powerful and poetic witness to the life, death, and resurrection of Jesus Christ. Yet the temptations in the wilderness, the Last Supper, the confession and resignation of Gethsemane are missing. Still, the Gospel of John provides timely lessons for life and faith for modern times. Instead of the short, pithy moral teachings and religious instructions (including parables and proverbs) concerning Mosaic law found in the Synoptics, the Gospel of John is marked by Jesus speaking long discourses and engaging in lengthy debates with his enemies. Many of these conversations focus on the validity of his messiahship and relationship to God. Jesus' enemies are often identified as "the Jews," although the Gospel does not define exactly who these people are. Indeed, the Gospel presents Jesus himself as a Jewish native of Nazareth. Nonetheless, the designation of those who oppose Jesus as "the Jews" sets up the conflict between those who believe in Jesus as the Messiah and those who do not. It is important, therefore, that we modern readers of the Gospel not use this book to promote anti-Semitism. It is tempting to identify

Jewish people corporately with "the Jews" of John, but they
are probably not the same people. We must avoid making an
easy mark of persons of our day by assuming they are de-
scended from "the Jews" who are unidentified by John.

Passages from this book are quite familiar but often misunderstood. There are many references to passages in the Hebrew Scriptures. There are allusions to previous passages and
passages yet to come in the Gospel itself. There are "insider"
allusions to life in the new community of the Word and the
Spirit which result from the coming of Christ. The people with
whom Jesus talks are often portrayed as dim-witted: they look
without seeing; they listen without hearing; they question without understanding. Jesus and the people seem always to be
talking at cross-purposes. They seem never quite to understand Jesus. Even his own disciples have difficulty fully understanding his teaching and his actions.

In this Gospel, God is mostly referred to in masculine terms.
Male images of God can be painful for many women because
they are a reminder of the oppression of patriarchy. It is true
that exclusive male language narrows our concept of God and
perpetuates systems of oppression. However, in John's Gospel, "Father" is a crucial name for God and to change the language would be to distort greatly its meaning both in its original context and what it could mean for us. Our task, therefore,
is to discern what the biblical writer and the early church were
trying to convey through these images of God. John stresses
throughout the book the close relationship between Jesus and
God. By referring to God as "Father" and to Jesus as "Son,"
John wants to convey a sense of intimacy and kinship. His goal
is not to reinforce patriarchal concerns; it is to concretize a
wonderfully mysterious relationship. We will work hard to keep
John's intention in mind as we examine our selected texts.

Further, there is an inherent dualism in the structure of
this Gospel: contrasts are made between light and darkness;

flesh and spirit; believers and nonbelievers; and good and evil. Some parts of this Gospel are confusing, some parts are overly repetitive. Jesus begins almost all of his speeches with the formula, "Very truly, I say to you." At points, Jesus seems to go on and on with explanations; sometimes long discourses make the arguments more obscure rather than making them clearer. Despite these difficulties, the Gospel has a structure that conveys meaning and purpose. Like each of the other three Gospels, John's work represents the mtempt of a particular community, working through a scribe or group of scribes, to record traditions about Jesus. This Gospel's aim is to proclaim who Jesus is and to persuade all to believe in him as God's Messiah.

The Gospel of John is used sparingly in the lectionary, which is a fixed selection of readings from the Old and New Testaments to be read and heard in local church worship services. In the church's three-year lectionary cycle, each of the Synoptics has its own year: Matthew is Year A; Mark is Year B; and Luke is Year C. There is no year for John! John's Gospel is not often heard in the preaching and teaching of the church, yet it is preached during Christmas, Lent, and Easter. Passages from John are used to complement other Gospel texts rather than as independent preaching and teaching sources. However, John guides us through the important turning points of our faith story: the celebration of Jesus' birth, the preparation for Jesus' death, and the joy of Jesus' resurrection. This Bible study resource is designed to enhance and deepen your understanding of John's Gospel as well as your own lenten journey.

With all the difficulties that the Gospel of John presents, you may be wondering why we are even attempting this study. It is precisely because of its difficulties! This Gospel represents so much that is true about life. The Christian journey is not a well-mapped trip. We do not start at point A and arrive unruffled at point Z. Rather, the Christian journey is more like an odyssey or an extended adventure. There are twists, turns, detours, and forks in the road. There are encounters with travail, loneliness, misunderstanding, uncertainty, and doubt along the way. There are mountains to be scaled, rivers to be forded, and wild things to overcome. There are some clear paths and some new ones to be forged. It has been said that the easy route teaches us nothing. The Christian journey is an expert teacher!

Do not become dismayed if this book and our time together do not answer all your questions or solve all your problems. Our purpose is to walk together as we travel along this path, and getting there is half the fun! We will use the Gospel of John because it will challenge us while it consoles us. It will stimulate our thinking as it reassures us. It will push us as it comforts us.

My own life has been shaped by contrasts. Although I am a lifelong urban dweller, my family roots go back to rural Alabama. My family and I would return to Demopolis several times each year during my childhood. And the contrasts between the city and the country were startling! The 1950s and 1960s were very different from today. In the city, we had many conveniences: gas stoves, electric lights, stereo record players and tape players, paved streets, indoor plumbing, and public transportation. In the country, we had wood-burning stoves for cooking and heat, kerosene lamps for light, wind-up Victrolas (an "ancient," nonelectric record player and precursor to cassette tape decks and compact-disc players), gravel roads, and outhouses. In the city, we shopped at well-stocked supermarkets, where we found clean vegetables, cut and wrapped meats, and canned goods—all in one place. In the country, we ate what we raised—vegetables that grew in well-tended gardens, milk fresh from cows, eggs fresh from chickens, butter churned from fresh milk, meats from animals raised or hunted, and foods canned by homemakers. Before electricity changed things in Demopolis, we bought blocks of ice from a traveling iceman, put them in a box that looked like a primitive refrigerator (it was fittingly called an "icebox"), and doled out the precious commodity for lemonade while the rest kept foodstuffs cool. Those were the days!

In addition to fond memories of a simpler life, I have memories of an ugly Demopolis. Jim Crow and legal segregation prevailed. Our trips to Demopolis were during the pre–Rosa Parks, Martin Luther King Jr., and civil-rights days. As late as the mid-1960s, Demopolis was marred by signs of American apartheid: in restaurants and in train stations, there were signs that read "Colored" designating separate—but supposedly equal—sections for African Americans. Even at a young age, I knew that separate was never equal. I remember our long car rides to Demopolis from Chicago, wandering from gas station to gas station. My father refused to buy gas at those stations that did not permit us to use the restrooms. Many along the way did not!

I remember driving past restaurants and motels, hungry and tired, but knowing that we could not stop. It was always with relief that we arrived safely at our relatives' homes. The trip was long and sometimes humiliating, but somehow we made it. My father was smart, and his dignity and savvy always made for safe journeys.

I remember the long train rides. Because we were not allowed in the dining car, we carried with us shoe boxes filled with foods that traveled well—fresh fruit, fried chicken, and pound cake. The discomforts of the trip always seemed worthwhile because we arrived at homes where we were loved and welcomed. Our visits were occasions for celebrations, and we were shown indescribable hospitality by everyone we visited. And, of course, the return home was always good!

My urban comforts were balanced by rural experiences. My life has been shaped by both worlds. The writer of the Gospel of John uses similar contrasts to make his point, which is that belief and faith in Jesus Christ make the ultimate relationship. Throughout the Gospel, there are conflicts between those who believe in God through Jesus and those who do not. There are conflicts between those who see and those who do not. There are conflicts between those who hear and those who do not. John's mission is to persuade persons that Jesus is God's Chosen One and God's fulfillment to bring salvation and eternal life to the world. John is clear in his theology and makes few attempts to reconcile the contrasts and conflicts.

The images in the Gospel and in our study are familiar to some and will be new to others. I will draw upon my urban and rural experiences in these studies to help illustrate what the biblical witnesses knew. This Bible study resource will serve as a reminder for some of you, and an introduction for others, of bygone days when life was limited by circumstances not of our making and of days that were rich and joyous. I will talk a lot about my experiences in Demopolis, those in the Middle East, where I visited in 1992, and those in Chicago. These experiences have shaped my worldview, my thinking, and my values. Further, this resource will challenge you to stretch out and to dig deep within as you encounter, again and anew, the country preacher from Galilee—the one who worked as a carpenter and loved persons troubled in head, heart, body, and soul; the one who continues to love those of us who believe in and follow him. This Jesus of Nazareth, the risen Savior, consoled those of his day who sought peace and continues to console those of us who are harried, hurried, and hurt.

In this Gospel, we hear Jesus speaking to the conditions of our living—political, social, and spiritual. The Old South has given way to fuller integration; country ways have been abandoned; the "Colored" signs are long forgotten; people treat one another with greater respect. There is still work to be done, both in the South and in the North; our problems of racism and discrimination have not ended. But we have made steps. So it is with the church today. Two thousand years after Jesus walked the earth, things have changed, but there is still work to do. We still struggle to be the church that Jesus founded—one that is inclusive, loving, and mission-oriented. Our problems, both within and beyond the church, have not ended. But we are making steps. There is much to be learned from our triumphs and from our stumblings!

For the next seven weeks, we will look at the "I am" sayings of Jesus in the Gospel of John. It will help to read John's Gospel in its entirety before beginning this study. This will provide a panoramic view of the story and invite the reader into the suspense and drama of the journey that Jesus makes. After an initial reading, we will then examine seven sayings of Jesus:

- "I am the bread of life."
- "I am the light of the world."
- "I am the door for the sheep."
- "I am the good shepherd."
- "I am the resurrection and the life."
- "I am the way, and the truth, and the life."
- "I am the true vine."

The symbols used in these sayings are ones familiar to natives of Palestine. All are connected to the life that Jesus is and gives to believers. Some are foreign to us and will need explanation. Therefore, each study unit consists of an overview of the text, a meditation based on the text, reflection questions, and a short concluding prayer. You will need a Bible, preferably the New Revised Standard Version (NRSV), and a journal in which to record your thoughts, especially if you use *Bread of Life* as an individual study guide. It will help to pray before beginning each study, asking God for guidance, support, and illumination.

One of my chores during our visits to Demopolis was to pump water for cooking, drinking, and bathing, because we had no indoor plumbing. The first time I tried, I took my bucket outside and placed it under the nozzle of the pump. I grasped the handle and pumped and pumped and pumped—with no result. I could hear the suction of the pump, but no water came up or out. I was angry and frustrated and anxious because I was not accomplishing my chore, and I was embarrassed to say so. Finally, my uncle asked why I was taking so long to bring in the water. I replied that I had been pumping for a long time, but no water was coming forth. He asked if I had primed the pump. He explained that in order for the water to flow, I needed to pour a small amount of water into the pump before I started pumping. This water would help bring the water up from the well. I did as he instructed, and the pumping produced clear, cool, fresh water!

This resource serves as a primer for your pump of faith—just enough to get your spiritual juices flowing. It is my fervent prayer that you will use this as a step toward a deepened life of faith and study. In these pages, I will share my life and my faith, and I hope that my sharing will stimulate your own thinking and sharing. For the next seven weeks, we will journey together to that place where we encounter Christ Jesus, and may we

> speak God's wisdom, secret and hidden, which God decreed before the ages for our glory. None of the rulers of this age understood this; for if they had, they would not have crucified the God of glory. But, as it is written,
>
> > "What no eye has seen, nor ear heard,
> > nor the human heart conceived,
> > what God has prepared for those
> > who love God"—

these things God has revealed to us through the Spirit; for the Spirit searches everything, even the depths of God. (1 Cor. 2:7–10)

The apostle Paul penned these words to a gifted but troubled church in Corinth. The Corinthian church was situated near the center of one of the most important cities in Greece. Members of the Christian church were dealing with divisions and disorders within the congregation. Paul reminded them of their common hope and common faith. It is fitting that the modern church remember its roots during Lent. It is fitting that we revisit our faith journey during Lent. It is fitting that we take the time to experience Jesus again. It is fitting that we confirm our faith in and love for God!

WHO IS "I AM"?

Who is "I am"? It seems a simple thing to say who one is! I am Barbara Jean Essex. My name, however, does not tell you much about who I am. Only by spending quality time with me would you begin to understand who I am. It is the same with God! We can know things about God, but only real experience will enable us to glimpse what God is really like. As we read the Scripture, we see how others have experienced God:

- For Abram (later, Abraham), God was the voice pushing him and his family from the comforts of retirement to new frontiers in a strange land.
- For Hagar, God was a presence of strength and survival in an abusive and exploitive household.
- For Joseph, God was a rescuer who delivered him from a pit and prison and elevated him to "somebodiness" in Pharaoh's palace.
- For Esther, God was an expert strategist who made a way out of no way and enabled her to save her people from massacre.

- For Jeremiah, God was a fire shut up in his bones.
- For Ezekiel, God was a surgeon and triage team who brought new life to dried bones.

Throughout the ages, women and men have tried to share their experiences of God, and their witness helps us to glimpse God. But only we, each of us, can tell what and who God is for us. We each experience God differently—God remains the same, but our understanding of God changes as we grow and live through life's joys and sorrows. Our experiences of God do not define the Divine—they merely give us glimpses of what God can be when our hearts and minds are open. It is not surprising, then, that when God reveals God's self, we are left puzzled:

> But Moses said to God, "If I come to the Israelites and say to them, 'The God of your ancestors has sent me to you,' and they ask me, 'What is God's name?' what shall I say to them?" God said to Moses, "I AM WHO I AM." God said further, "Thus you shall say to the Israelites, 'I AM has sent me to you.'" God also said to Moses, "Thus you shall say to the Israelites, 'The . . . God of your ancestors, the God of Abraham, the God of Isaac, and the God of Jacob, has sent me to you':
>
> > This is my name forever,
> > and this my title for all
> > generations." (Exod. 3:13–15)

Throughout the Hebrew Scriptures, the phrase "I am" is most often used to designate the divine. God declares:

- "I am . . . the God of Abraham your father and the God of Isaac" (Gen. 28:13).
- "I am the God who heals you" (Exod. 15:26).

- "I, I am God, and besides me there is no savior" (Isa. 43:11).
- "I am . . . your God" (Ezek. 20:7).

God's nature and majesty are emphasized in the above texts and others like them. God reveals something of the divine character. God is Presence, Healer, Savior, and Keeper. God is the rock, the refuge, the protection that people seek. Likewise, self-disclosures of Jesus tell us something about him as well as expanding our understanding of God.

We are struck by the number of times the phrase "I am" (Greek: *ego eimi*) occurs in the Gospel of John. It is uttered twenty-nine times; of those, Jesus speaks the phrase twenty-six times. He uses seven predicates (one of the two main parts of a sentence, modifying the subject and including the verb, objects, or phrases governed by the verb): bread; light; door; shepherd; resurrection and life; way, truth, and life; and vine. These are images that his audience would know and understand; they carry social and religious meanings. By stating "I am," Jesus uses tangible symbols and images to help the people understand his authority and power. Some refused to accept his self-disclosure, and conflict resulted in his death. When Jesus utters "I am," he connects himself with the God of the Hebrew Scriptures, made known to the Israelites in their deliverance from bondage in Egypt. The divinity of Jesus is grounded in God. The humanity of Jesus is centered in the incarnation—God's Word made flesh and living in our midst. This mystery is made manifest in the ways in which Jesus behaved and labeled himself. By seeing the spiritual significance in everyday images, Jesus helps us to experience God in meaningful and deep ways.

Jesus uses the "I am" phrase to express his identity: "Very truly, I tell you, before Abraham was, I am" (John 8:58). Jesus establishes identity with God as a child to a parent. The writer

of this Gospel makes sure that Jesus' identity is clear right from
the very beginning:

> In the beginning was the Word, and the Word was with God,
> and the Word was God. Jesus was in the beginning with God.
> All things came into being through the Word, and without
> the Word not one thing came into being. What has come into
> being in the Word was life, and the life was the light of all
> people. The light shines in the shadows, and the shadows did
> not overcome it. (John 1:1–5)

While the Synoptics begin with Jesus' earthly genealogy,
John begins with his heavenly origins. Throughout the Gospel, Jesus fleshes out (pun intended!) who he is. He uses con-
crete images and familiar concepts to help the people see who
he is. Truly seeing, according to John's theology, should lead
to belief and discipleship.

Jesus is the self-expression of God, because Jesus claims ultimate intimacy with God. In the Gospel of John, Jesus is God's
final revelation. Jesus comes from above and fully shows us
who God is and what God is like. Jesus is the tangible, public
side of God. John emphasizes the divinity of Jesus throughout
the Gospel to show that this one is God's fulfillment of promises made to the saints of Israel.

Ultimately, although we will learn things about Jesus, we
will have to have experiences with him to truly know him. Jesus
invites us to encounter him; he seeks our companionship. To
facilitate the process, Jesus asked a lot of questions of those
who would follow him:

- "What are you looking for?" (John 1:38).
- "Are you a teacher of Israel, and yet you do not understand
  these things?" (John 3:9–10).
- "Do you want to be made well?" (John 5:6).

- "Do you also wish to go away?" (John 6:66–67).
- "Why are you looking for an opportunity to kill me?" (John 7:19–20).
- "Do you know what I have done to you?" (John 13:12–15).
- "Why are you weeping? Whom are you looking for?" (John 20:15).
- "Do you love me?" (John 21:15–17).

Jesus' questions are challenging and difficult. His most piercing question was and remains, "Who do you say that I am?" In the end, our answer to this question is the one that counts. I pray that this resource will help you answer with bold conviction, "You are the Messiah, the Child of the living God!" (see Matt. 16:13–20).

CLOSING PRAYER

Eternal God, we come before you trembling. We are fearful of, yet grateful for, the journey that lies ahead of us. We pray for your Spirit to accompany us—to calm our fears and push our thinking, so that we may see you more clearly and love Jesus more deeply. In Christ's name, we pray. Amen.

SESSION 2

THE BREAD OF LIFE

Bible Study
"I am the bread of life."

Read John 6:25–40

Jesus said to them, "I am the bread of life. Whoever comes to me will never be hungry, and whoever believes in me will never be thirsty." *(John 6:36)*

Begin with prayer

OVERVIEW

IN JOHN 5, Jesus heals a lame man on the Sabbath. His act of healing leads to a long debate with "the Jews," an unidentified group of people who oppose Jesus throughout the Gospel. After communication fails, Jesus and his disciples travel to the eastern shore of the Sea of Galilee, where they are followed by a large crowd.

The feeding of the five thousand (see John 6:1–14) is a miracle story that appears in all four Gospels (see Matthew 14:13–21, 15:32–39; Mark 6:30–44, 8:1–10; and Luke 9:10–17). Jesus anticipates the needs of the crowd and asks Philip where they can buy food to feed the crowd. Both Philip and Andrew see that they lack the resources to satisfy the people's needs. The disciples do not have the six months' wages needed to buy enough food; they have only five loaves of barley bread and two fish. The count of five thousand does not include women and children; the actual crowd probably was three times as large.

After the disciples instruct the people to sit down, Jesus presides over a simple meal: he takes the loaves and fish, gives thanks to God, and distributes the food to the people. The leftovers are gathered, and they fill twelve baskets. After this miracle meal, the people declare Jesus a prophet and seek to make him king.

Not wanting the office, Jesus withdraws to the mountains to be alone. The disciples, who have stayed behind, attempt to cross the sea to Capernaum to join him. As a storm arises, they are terrified. They look up to see Jesus walking on the water. This second miracle is recorded only in Matthew (14:22–32), Mark (6:45–51), and John (6:16–21). In all three, it follows the feeding miracle. Jesus identifies himself (the Greek is *ego eimi,* literally, "I am"). The New Revised Standard Version translates the phrase "It is I," but the appropriate translation is "I am." This designation goes back to the God of the Hebrew Scriptures, who is revealed to Moses. With the presence of Jesus, the disciples safely reach the shore.

The next day, the crowd arrives by crossing the sea in boats. They ask Jesus how he has gotten there, since they did not see him in the boat with his disciples (John 6:25). Their question is a natural one; they are curious about Jesus' movement. But their question is ironic because it reveals that they do not know Jesus. In the opening chapter of this Gospel, John states that Jesus has always been here—in the beginning and even before Abraham. The people do not know what they are asking, nor do they understand what they are seeing!

Instead of answering their question, Jesus launches into a lengthy discourse about their motives. Jesus tells them that they seek him because their physical hunger has been satisfied and not because they see God's hand in the feeding miracle. Jesus challenges them to seek food that provides eternal life.

The people do not understand (a recurring motif), and they ask what works they should perform to receive this special bread. Jesus tries to explain by telling them that the work of God is to believe in Jesus, the one sent by God. The people still do not understand. They ask Jesus for a sign to verify that he is, indeed, the one sent by God. Further, they demand that Jesus provide a sign that surpasses that of Moses, who provided manna to their ancestors in the wilderness.

In exasperation, Jesus explains that it was not Moses who provided the life-sustaining manna from heaven—it was God! Only God gives true sustenance, and the true bread is life to the world. The people's response indicates that they still do not quite understand: "Sir, give us this bread always" (John 6:34).

Jesus declares, "I am the bread of life." He continues, "Whoever comes to me will never be hungry, and whoever believes in me will never be thirsty." The people, however, cannot see Jesus' divinity; they know him as a human being, with human parents. Some probably have watched him grow up; others may have bought wares from his carpentry shop. Therefore, they complain that this person whom they know cannot possibly have come down from heaven.

Jesus continues the debate: the mystery of belief is initiated by God, and humanity must respond. Jesus tells them that anyone who believes in him can do so only because God has willed it. Jesus quotes the prophets, knowing that if the people are paying attention, they will recognize Jesus as God's Messiah.

Jesus goes on to say that their ancestors ate manna and died. But Jesus is the living bread that gives eternal life. In verses 52–65, Jesus makes eucharistic claims: anyone who eats his flesh and drinks his blood will have a new relationship with God as well as eternal life!

In this episode, Jesus and the crowd use the same words, but the meanings differ greatly. The people are willing only to deal with the tangible, literal feeding of their physical hunger. They seek a sign as proof of Jesus' claim of intimacy with God. They see Jesus only as the offspring of Joseph and Mary. They miss the mark on several levels. First, the people want a sign of God's presence. Although they have witnessed the miracle meal and have eaten their fill, they do not recognize the miracle as a sign! They fail to realize that a sign, any sign, points to someone or something beyond itself. In our faith, signs are willed and intended by God. The people already have been given a sign, but they do not see it.

Second, the people misinterpret their own faith history. Impressed by wonder-working, they think that Moses called down manna from heaven to feed their ancestors. Again, the manna was a sign that God was providing for God's people. Moses had no powers of his own, except those given to him by God. Again, they fail to see the sign.

Third, the people cannot see beyond the tangible. They are stumped by Jesus' claim to be the bread of life because they think they know him. No doubt, some of them remember the circumstances of his birth. Many know Joseph and Mary. Some probably saw Jesus as a toddler, an adolescent, or as a teenager working in Joseph's carpentry shop. They cannot understand how someone they already know can now be this special servant of God. They are hung up on earthly genealogy and cannot really see Jesus. They cannot see Jesus as an object of faith.

The people speak and understand things literally, while Jesus puts a spiritual spin on their conversation. This confusion heightens the tension of the story as it moves toward its inevitable end at the empty tomb. The people seek bread that nourishes for a little while; Jesus offers himself for all time and for eternity.

Jesus brings an end to all hunger and thirst. Physical hunger is only a shadow of the deep hunger of the human soul. Jesus recognizes this hunger among the people: they have lived in great expectation of God's Messiah, who will come, they hope, to fix their lives. The people are oppressed, despised, and exploited by the ruling powers of the day. Further, they are sick in limb and heart. They are hungry for peace, hungry for joy, hungry for love, hungry for justice. Many have claimed to have the answer for the people; they have been tricked and disappointed before. Therefore, they want to be sure that this Jesus is truly the one sent by God and not just another charlatan.

They had thought that John the Baptist was the Messiah. He assured them that he was not. He told them that God's Messiah was on the way and in their midst. But the people look at Jesus and see just an ordinary man, and a carpenter at that. He defies their vision of a warrior-king who will overthrow the Roman authorities. Jesus, with his callused hands, does not fit their image of the mighty deliverer who will restore Israel to military and political glory.

Jesus does some wonderful things, to be sure—he heals the lame, gives sight to the blind, and even feeds the hungry. He teaches some marvelous lessons: human life and wholeness are important, even on the Sabbath. But the people want to be sure!

Although all the signs are there, the people just do not see them! They look but do not see; they listen but do not hear. Their failure results in disbelief. John makes very clear that those who do not see cannot believe and therefore have no place in the community. There is no room for wavering: if you see, you must believe.

Jesus knows that "true bread" is not the manna in the wilderness; nor is it the miracle of the barley loaves. The "true bread" is Christ Jesus, who makes the way for a new relationship with God. It is God who gives and sustains life. Indeed, Jesus gives his own life to make this relationship possible. Jesus tells the people that all of their needs, religious and human, are satisfied through belief in him—because Jesus and God are one!

MEDITATION

In the 1950s and 1960s, my family and I traveled by car from Chicago to Demopolis, Alabama. Because of racial discrimination and segregation, there were few places along the way where we could stop to eat. This was an era before fast-food chains and highway rest stops existed. It is hard to imagine it now: miles and miles of two-lane roads rather than today's superhighways; miles and miles of fields and pastures rather than today's entrance and exit ramps; miles and miles of billboards rather than the clean, airy franchise restaurants where travelers stop to eat today.

We had to pack lunches with foods that did not require refrigeration. We packed boxes of fresh fruit, raw vegetables, fried chicken, cake, and always loaves of bread! We could make a nourishing and filling meal with some fruit, veggies, a little meat, and some bread. When it came to bread, a little bit went a long way.

Even today, bread is a dietary staple that provides nourishment. It is a sign of hospitality and communion to break bread with others. Bread has been called the staff of life and is one of the basic staples of life. Bread can be made from all kinds of grains; it can be flat or raised. Bread can be baked or cooked on a griddle. Every culture has some kind of bread—it is a universal food.

Bread figures prominently in the Bible: there are several religious rites that use bread (including the Passover, the Feast of the Unleavened Bread, and the Bread of the Presence); several cereal offerings are based on breads and grains; and the Eucharist, or Holy Communion, may be the most familiar to us.

Bread sustains and nourishes life. Life is more than physical existence; real life results in a new relationship with God, a quality of life that includes trust, obedience, and love. This new life is made possible by Jesus Christ. Without Jesus, we can have existence, but only Jesus gives real life.

Jesus, as the bread of life, satisfies all of our hungers—today, tomorrow, and for all eternity. Jesus is our sustenance;

whatever our hunger, Jesus satisfies! In this sixth chapter of John's Gospel, we learn the valuable lesson that in Christ, our hunger and thirst are satisfied. Further, in life and beyond, we are safe because Jesus is the "I am."

During the period of Lent, let us take time to "see" the Jesus who is, not the one we wish existed. When Jesus healed the sick and fed the hungry, he challenged them: "Follow me!"

Like our biblical sisters and brothers, we, too often, say, "Not yet." Jesus challenged them and challenges us to *see, believe, and follow!* A modern cynic has said that we are to believe none of what we hear and only half of what we see. Jesus, however, brings a different perspective. When it comes to Jesus, WYSIWYG: what you see is what you get! Seeing and believing are part and parcel of John's understanding of faith. The people's demand for a sign shows that they looked without seeing; that they experienced without understanding. How can we see and not believe?

We have the responsibility of choosing whether we will believe. Jesus is God's gift to the world. Can you see him? Do you believe? Are you willing to follow?

QUESTIONS FOR REFLECTION

1. The image of hunger is familiar and historical: the Israelites were hungry and thirsty in the wilderness; Jesus began his ministry with a forty-day fast; the early church held public fasts during Lent and other holy times. Jesus saw fasting as service to God, an indication of true conversion, and frequently as an accompaniment to prayer.

   For what do you hunger and thirst? Explain.

   How might fasting, as a spiritual discipline, help satisfy your hunger and thirst?

   How is Jesus the bread of life for you? How does Jesus satisfy your needs?

2. The unnamed lad in the feeding miracle had five barley loaves. Barley bread was the least expensive of all breads; it was the bread of the very poor.

   What are the implications for our efforts to alleviate hunger in the world to know that Jesus fed the masses with the bread of the poor?

   What happens when we bring our meager gifts to Jesus?

   What do you have to offer Jesus? to your congregation? to your community? Explain.

3. The Eucharist (Holy Communion) was the last meal Jesus shared with his disciples before his death. The sharing of meals was a distinctive characteristic of Jesus' ministry— he often broke bread with unlikely tablemates. In the early church, the meal was a centerpiece of community and was rooted in the hope for the new age inaugurated by the risen and exalted Christ. The bread and wine of the Eucharist were connected to the redemptive act of Jesus' death and resurrection. Those who share the meal of the Eucharist are bound to one another by a common faith and hope.

   What does Holy Communion mean to and for you?

   What do you think about when you eat the bread and drink the wine during Holy Communion?

   How might the Eucharist help the church overcome its internal conflicts and divisions? Explain.

CLOSING PRAYER

Eternal and loving God, we thank you that you have not left us hungry and thirsty. You hear our cries for nourishment, and you answer by sending the bread that satisfies for all time. We claim Jesus as the Bread of Heaven, and our earnest prayer is this simple request: Bread of Heaven, feed us until we want no more. Amen.

THE LIGHT OF THE WORLD

Bible Study
"I am the light of the world."

Read John *8:12–30*

Again Jesus spoke to them, "I am the light of the world. Who-
ever follows me will never walk in shadows but will have the
light of life."   *(John 8:12)*

Begin with prayer

❖

OVERVIEW

THIS SAYING OF JESUS occurs in the midst of a long, troubling argument that begins in chapter 7. The setting for chap-
ters 7 and 8 is Jerusalem during the Feast of Booths (or Tab-
ernacles), one of three major pilgrimage festivals of Judaism
(the others are the Passover and the Festival of Weeks, or Pen-
tecost). The Festival of Booths was a joyous harvest celebration. The people set up tents or booths and lived in them for
eight days to remember God's protection while Israel wandered in the wilderness (see Lev. 23:39–43).

The conflict between Jesus and his unidentified "Jewish"
opposition heightens in this series of short episodes. Jesus
makes bold claims about his identity, and the officials plot
against him. The officials set out to test Jesus by demanding
that he rightly interpret Mosaic law. Jesus either refuses to
play their game or plays their game to their disadvantage. Especially poignant is the story of the woman caught in the act
of adultery (John 8:2–11). The "scribes and Pharisees" ask Jesus
what they should do, since Mosaic law requires that they stone
the woman to death.

Instead of answering their question, Jesus bends down and writes in the dirt. His action indicates his refusal to interact with them. The officials continue to ply Jesus with their questions. Finally, Jesus stands up and challenges anyone without sin to throw the first stone. Then he bends down and writes in the dirt, again indicating his refusal to deal with them. When he stands up a third time, only the woman remains; the others have walked away—even the elders, the pillars of the community. Jesus offers the woman an opportunity for a fresh start; he does not hold her past against her.

The remarkable aspect of this story is the way in which Jesus deals with the trap. Jesus maintains control by ignoring their ploy. When he speaks, he addresses the officials and the woman as equal sinners. He provides an opportunity for all of them to break from the old ways and to embrace God's new world order—an order characterized by forgiveness and fresh starts. Jesus uses his internal, heaven-given authority to butt heads with the religious establishment.

It seems like a small thing to us; but for the people of his day, Jesus' behavior was radical! It is important for us to understand that "the Jews" were searching desperately for the Messiah, but their idea of the Messiah was that of a superior political and military power. They were not expecting a humble carpenter who doled out forgiveness and second chances. They were expecting a Messiah to be on their side, not a man who provided new insights into traditions they had long held sacred.

Jesus violates the Sabbath, engages in a theological discussion with a Samaritan woman, and makes bold claims about himself. Jesus urges the people to stop judging themselves and one another by human standards. Judgment belongs to God, because only God knows enough to judge rightly.

Jesus says, "I am the light of the world!" In many cultures and religions, light is a symbol for the divine. In the Hebrew Scriptures, light figures prominently as a manifestation of God:

- "God went in front of them in a pillar of cloud by day, to lead them along the way, and in a pillar of fire by night, to give them light, so that they might travel by day and by night." (Exod. 13:21)
- "God is my light and my salvation; whom shall I fear? God is the stronghold of my life; of whom shall I be afraid?" (Ps. 27:1).
- "O send out your light and your truth; let them lead me; let them bring me to your holy hill and to your dwelling" (Ps. 43:3).
- "Your word is a lamp to my feet and a light to my path" (Ps. 119:105).
- "O house of Jacob, come, let us walk in the light of God!" (Isa. 2:5).
- "The people who walked in shadows have seen a great light; those who lived in a land of deep shadows—on them light has shined" (Isa. 9:2).
- "Do not rejoice over me, O my enemy; when I fall, I shall rise; when I sit in shadows, God will be a light to me" (Mic. 7:8).

Light is seen as evidence of God's presence and protection as well as God's judgment and mercy. Jesus' claim goes all the way back to the beginning of creation. God's first act was to create light (see Gen. 1:3–4). To establish the connection between God's word, John states early in the Gospel: "All things came into being through the Word, and without the Word not one thing came into being. What has come into being in the Word was life, and the life was the light of all people. The light shines in the shadows, and the shadows did not overcome it" (John 1:3–5). Jesus provides the light that overcomes those things that work against wholeness, peace, unity, and love.

Jesus reveals himself as the light of the world and makes a judgment on the Feast of Booths. Light was an essential part of the celebration: four large lamp stands were lit at the end of the first day of the feast. It is said that these four lamp stands produced so much light that all the courtyards in Jerusalem basked in their brilliance. Jesus declares that he is the fulfillment of what the Feast of Booths commemorates. The lamp stands light Jerusalem, but Jesus lights the entire world even brighter than that! Jesus, as light, forces persons to decide: to see the light is to follow Jesus; refusal to see the light results in walking in the absence of light.

The Greek word translated "follow" (*akolouthein*) is a term of discipleship. It involves total commitment to the one who is both teacher and Messiah. This act of discipleship includes both salvation and suffering. Even though the way is uncharted and fraught with dangers, Jesus assures his followers that they will not stumble. The path is lit by the one who is the ultimate light, and that light also gives life.

Jesus' declaration that he is the light of the world leads to a nasty exchange with the "scribes and Pharisees." They ask pointed and testy questions: "Who are you?" (John 8:25) and "Who do you claim to be?" (John 8:53). But they do not like the answer Jesus gives in John 8:58–59: "Very truly, I tell you, before Abraham was, I am." So they pick up stones to throw at him, but Jesus hides himself and goes out of the temple.

This eighth chapter of John is one of the more difficult passages of Scripture! The Jesus portrayed here defies most of what we think we know of him. Here, Jesus viciously attacks his opponents again and again. The Jesus we are used to is humble and meek: he eats with outcasts and sinners; he heals lepers and those with withered hands; he raises the dead and stops the flow of blood in ailing women; he seeks lost coins and sheep; he feeds the multitude; he forgives those who are repentant.

The Jesus in this eighth chapter directs his venom against a group labeled "the Jews." This chapter has been the basis of much discussion about Christian anti-Semitism. If we are to be true to the intent of the text, we must take the time to recapture as much as we can of the original context and function of the discourse for its original audience. Then and only then can we decide what lessons the passage holds for us today.

Scholars generally agree that late in the first century of the Christian era, there was a split from the synagogue. Before the break, John's Christians practiced aspects of Judaism as well as exercising their faith in Jesus. This dual allegiance caused some tension: the synagogue was where the Scripture was heard and taught. There was a need to keep the faith pure. The life of the community was governed by the words of God through the saints and prophets of the Hebrew Scriptures. (Remember that for Jesus, the Hebrew Scriptures were the whole Scripture; there was no New Testament until after his death!) Whenever there were conflicts or decisions to be made, the elders appealed to the Scriptures—it was the definitive arbiter of justice and decision-making for the adherents of Judaism.

Christians in John's community saw Jesus as the fulfillment of the Scriptures—Jesus was the Messiah! When the prophets spoke of one chosen by God to deliver the people, they spoke of Jesus. When the Scriptures spoke of the suffering servant, they spoke of Jesus. The synagogue did not believe this. Jesus just did not fit the mold; he was everything the people did not want. The synagogue required indisputable proof that Jesus was the one. Thus, much of John's Gospel is designed to convince and persuade the synagogue that Jesus is God's Messiah. The allusions and references to the Hebrew Scriptures are not accidental; they are there to prove who Jesus is.

In addition, John makes several references to being cast out of the synagogue:

- "His parents said this because they were afraid of the Jews; for the Jews had already agreed that anyone who confessed Jesus to be the Messiah would be put out of the synagogue" (John 9:22).

- "Nevertheless many, even of the authorities, believed in Jesus. But because of the Pharisees they did not confess it, for fear that they would be put out of the synagogue; for they loved human glory more than the glory that comes from God" (John 12:42–43).
- "Jesus said, 'They will put you out of the synagogues. Indeed, an hour is coming when those who kill you will think that by doing so they are offering worship to God'" (John 16:2).

The threat of being cast out evoked great distress and anxiety for the people. It is important to note that for the descendants of Israel, community was everything. There was no life outside the community. People were identified by bloodlines and not as individuals. To be excommunicated was a fate worse than death. God delivered the tribes of Israel, and they saw themselves connected to one another in real and powerful ways. God related to them as a group, and to be cut off from the group was to be cut off from God! It was a serious matter for believers in the God of Abraham, Isaac, and Jacob to be outside the community.

John's Christians fervently believed that Jesus was the Messiah, and they cast themselves against their sisters and brothers in the synagogue, "the Jews." John's group was seen as a subversive group of misguided folks who blasphemed against God by believing in a carpenter from Nazareth. They were ridiculed and ostracized by their own relatives and faith community. John's Christians, then, saw themselves as outcasts, rejected, and cut off from the family within which their identity was based. They saw themselves as powerless victims of the dominant religious group of which they had been a part all their lives.

In John's Gospel, this now-oppressive group is called "the Jews." The group is obviously hostile toward Jesus and his followers—not because they are inherently bad people. "The Jews" are only attempting to keep their traditions intact and pure. They think they are correct in not falling for the claims of an itinerant preacher and healer: false prophets had appeared throughout Israel's history; Jesus could be another one! The goal of "the Jews" was not to hurt Jesus or his followers; if Jesus had gone quietly about his business, there would have been no need to deal with him at all.

However, Jesus' mission was public and challenged the basic tenets of Judaism. He had to be stopped. But Jesus would not stop or go quietly. He healed the sick on the Sabbath, the holy day of rest. He fraternized with sinners and women, forbidden for saints of the faith. He challenged the interpretation of Mosaic laws, which were sacred and irrefutable. Jesus went about his business boldly and captured people's imagination. He rekindled a dormant hope that God was active in the nation's life. He sparked the expectation that better times were ahead—not just for military or political powers.

In addition, Jesus awakened the personal power of the common folk. Those who had been afflicted their entire lives now danced and saw and lived in wholeness. Those who had been isolated and neglected now knew love and care. Those who lived in the shadows of shame and guilt now held their heads high, knowing that they had another chance. Those who mourned now rejoiced because they had been remembered by a loving and caring God. These are the ones who were cast out of the synagogues. These are the ones who were despised by "the Jews." This Gospel is the story of those who were cut off; it is not the story of the majority. This is the voice of those whose power is not of this world, so the world turned against it.

The vicious language of chapter 8 has as its backdrop the feeling of being cut off from one's roots. This is protest language against the religious and political power structures before which John's community was helpless. They had only rhetoric to unleash—they had no power to enforce their beliefs or to effect justice.

The issues emphasized in John 8—the interpretation of Mosaic law, the validity of witnesses to Jesus' identity, and historical and familial ties to Abraham—were family struggles for that time! It is a mistake to think that struggle mirrors modern conflicts. We cannot take the tone of chapter 8 and use it as a weapon against Judaism today. The situation of that time is totally different from today's. Christians now have an established place in the world. Nations formerly hostile to Christianity and where its practice was illegal and punishable by death now have a sizable Christian presence.

The function of John 8 for that Christian community was to bolster their self-esteem and to point out the error of non-believers. This was their weapon against the attack of the Jewish religious establishment. These Christians were seeking to justify their existence over and against the powers that had cut them off. They felt they had to reject those who had already rejected them. In other words, "You can't fire me! I quit!" Their fight, however, is not our fight.

Today's Christian church fights a different struggle. Today we are greatly concerned about dwindling congregational membership, diminishing financial giving, and decreasing interest in and support for mission. Today we wrestle with issues of pluralism, diversity, and inclusivity. Today we struggle with interfaith dialogues and with diverse faith communities. We would be well advised to use Scripture to guide us to healing and reconciliation rather than using it to lash out at those who are different from ourselves.

The conflict between the followers of Jesus and "the Jews" was a family squabble that escalated to tragic ends. Neither side was willing to compromise, and so the end was inevitable.

John's Gospel was intended to be "good news" for those who had been pushed out by their own sisters and brothers. John tells them that they are right and that Jesus will take care of them. Where they once lived without really knowing God, now they can know God because Jesus has been sent for that purpose. Where they once lived without hope for a viable future, now they can expect a meaningful future because Jesus has made the way. Where they once lived in shadows, now they can walk in the light because Jesus *is* the light—not just for this persecuted, outcast community, but for all people everywhere!

MEDITATION

When I was about seven years old, I went shopping with my paternal grandmother. We were in the Demopolis Woolworth store. I was thirsty and looked for a water fountain. I found two against a wall near the rear of the store. As I approached, I saw a white porcelain fountain that was stained and cluttered with paper, trash, and gum. The other was a modern aluminum fountain that was spotless and dispensed cool water. I took a sip from the aluminum fountain. At that instant, I heard my soft-spoken grandmother shriek, "Girl! Get away from there!" The tone and urgency of her voice frightened me. As I backed away from the fountain, I looked up and saw two signs. The one over the porcelain fountain read "Colored." The one over the aluminum fountain read "White." I asked my grandmother why she was so upset. She hushed me up and hustled me out of the store. She was obviously embarrassed and admonished me to always pay attention to those signs—my safety depended on it.

This incident is my first memory of being afraid, angry, and different! It was a few years before I fully understood the import of that sip of water. As I watched the events of the civil-rights movement unfold, I knew that a little sip of water could have sparked an incident in which my grandmother and I could have been bodily harmed. As I watched the water hoses and police dogs unleashed on innocent black children, women, and men, I knew that this country was deeply divided.

It was years before I learned to channel my anger in constructive ways. I spent most of my teenage and early college years spouting the rhetoric of the black-power movement. This movement—with its images of fire, death, and destruction—offered me a way to understand and vent my rage and hurt. I never took the opportunity to engage in violent retaliation; I do not know whether I could have done so. I engaged in mild protests and longed for a day when African Americans would be in power.

The "White" and "Colored" signs are down now. Even in South Africa, the signs are down. But the wounds caused by the signs and the meanings behind them remain. My own wounds are not completely healed, but I understand better now that there are systems—powers and principalities—that continue to oppress and exploit persons. I still cringe with rage when some well-meaning but unthinking white person refers to African Americans as "colored people." My own birth certificate, which I had amended to update the racial category, is a painful reminder of a tragic era; under race, my birth certificate says, "Colored."

These encounters with racism could have made me a bitter and unforgiving person. And for years I was. Fortunately, my parents and grandparents continued to insist that I attend church. There I heard the "songs of Zion," songs we sang in a strange land, which gave us strength and hope. There I heard the word of God preached, and learned about those who lived in a hope that present circumstances did not determine ultimate worth. There I learned that there is one who also was reviled and persecuted. There I learned that there is one who came from humble beginnings and changed the world. There I learned that there is one who understands my pain and keeps me in his care. There I learned that there is one who shows a different way of being in the world—despite the troubles in society. Jesus came into my life as light and showed me another way. My faith and belief in Jesus Christ have empowered me to work through my hurt and to work with others to make this a better society.

There is a resurgence of systemic racism in this country—hate groups are attacking and killing persons who are different; school systems are eliminating bilingual-education programs; universities and state governments are giving in to Affirmative Action backlash; xenophobic and homophobic "Christians" are casting out members who are different; greedy entrepreneurs are displacing the poor so that they can build luxury homes for the rich—and no one wins. Both the oppressed and the oppressor suffer. I imagine that Jesus weeps over us as he did over Jerusalem. We do not walk in the light that God provides through Jesus. Instead of being hospitable, we are hostile toward sisters and brothers because of their race, color, ethnicity, gender, or sexual orientation. Instead of reaching out to those who are lonely, afraid, and lost, we push them away and take for our selfish comfort the resources they need for survival.

There are persons throughout the land for whom there is no light. The light in many lives has been extinguished because of the suffering they endure personally and socially. It is to these that we must bring the light of Christ. Jesus is depending on us to bring light to those places and conditions that need illumination—greed, apathy, ignorance. Jesus is depending on us to let our lights shine so that others will know who it is we follow and why. Jesus is depending on us to let our lights shine so that hope, renewal, and redemption are possible.

Jesus is the light of the world. If we are his followers, we, too, have a light that must shine!

QUESTIONS FOR REFLECTION

1. Turning on a light in a room enables us to see what is there but does not change the character of the room.

    What in your life needs the light of Jesus? Explain.

    What conditions or situations in your congregation and/or community need light?

    What might you do to bring light to the situations and conditions you have identified in your congregation and/or community?

2. Jesus, as light, gives life, inviting the rejected into community. What does this mean in our context of religious pluralism and cultural diversity?

3. As we get older, we need more light to see and read. What are the spiritual implications of this physical change?

CLOSING PRAYER

Jesus, Light of the World, you give light and life. Let your light shine on us. Let your cleansing light expose our sins, known and unknown, and wipe them from our repentant hearts. Let your healing light bring restoration to our places of pain and devastation. Help us to reflect your light in those places where we have some influence. Empower us to be your lights wherever we find ourselves. And, Savior, let us bask in your love and light, that we might truly know your grace and mercy. Amen.

THE DOOR FOR THE SHEEP

Bible Study
"I am the door for the sheep."

Read John *10:1–10*

So again Jesus said to them, "Very truly, I tell you, I am the gate for the sheep."　　　　　　　　　(*John 10:7*)

Begin with prayer

━━━✕━━━

OVERVIEW

THIS TEXT SEEMS self-explanatory: it describes the relationship between a shepherd and sheep. The authentic shepherd enters the sheepfold by the door or gate; it is a public entrance with no tricks or deception. Those who enter by another way are thieves and bandits, and thus inauthentic. The true shepherd calls the sheep by name, and they respond because they know their shepherd's voice. All others are strangers because the sheep do not recognize their voices. The sheep will follow the true shepherd and not the stranger because they do not recognize the stranger's voice.

The Pharisees from chapter 9 do not understand (no surprise, right?). Jesus goes on to explain: Jesus is the "door" for the sheep and determines who goes in and who goes out. Those whom Jesus lets in are saved and safe. The pretenders—thieves and bandits—steal, kill, and destroy. Only Jesus gives life and gives abundant life.

This seems like a simple story on the surface. However, it echoes much from the Hebrew Scriptures. The shepherd is one who tends a flock of sheep or goats. Palestine is more conducive to sheepherding than to agriculture; it is not sur-

prising, therefore, that pastoral images are prominent in the
Hebrew Scriptures and are carried over in the New Testament.
The shepherd's work included leading the sheep to food and
water, keeping them safely sheltered, and keeping the flock
together. The shepherd also guarded the flock against thieves,
bandits, and wild animals.

Sheep are mentioned more than five hundred times in the
Bible, both as literal and figurative entities. Sheep have been
used as metaphors for human beings, and the shepherd has
symbolized God. God is the good shepherd who protects and
cares for the helpless:

- "You led your people like a flock by the hand of Moses
  and Aaron" (Ps. 77:20).
- "Know that the Sovereign is God. It is God that made us,
  and we are God's; we are God's people and the sheep of
  God's pasture" (Ps. 100:3).
- "God will feed God's flock like a shepherd; God will
  gather the lambs in God's arms, and carry them in God's
  bosom, and gently lead the mother sheep" (Isa. 40:11).
- "Woe to the shepherds who destroy and scatter the sheep
  of my pasture! says God. Therefore thus says the Sovereign, the God of Israel, concerning the shepherds who
  shepherd my people: It is you who have scattered my
  flock, and have driven them away, and you have not at-
  tended to them. So I will attend to you for your evil do-
  ings, says God. Then I myself will gather the remnant of
  my flock out of all the lands where I have driven them,
  and I will bring them back to their fold, and they shall be
  fruitful and multiply. I will raise up shepherds over them
  who will shepherd them, and they shall not fear any
  longer, or be dismayed, nor shall any be missing, says
  God" (Jer. 23:1–4).

John 10:1–10 emphasizes the close relationship between shepherd and flock. The sheep have total trust in the shepherd and are totally dependent on their leader. The shepherd loves the flock and calls each sheep by name.

Then, Jesus declares that he is the "gate" or "door" for the sheep. The New Revised Standard Version translates the Greek *thyra* as "gate." Technically, the translation should be "door." This word carries symbolic meaning; for instance, to "be at the door" means to be very near (see Mark 13:29), and to "open or close the door" means to accept or reject a special opportunity (see Matt. 7:7–8, Luke 11:9–10, and Acts 14:27).

The sheep are kept in a sheepfold. During biblical times, there were at least two kinds of sheepfolds. In the towns and villages, there were community sheepfolds where all the flocks were kept when grazing was done for the day. These were protected by a door with a lock, and the shepherd kept the key. The other type of sheepfold was used when the flocks were out on the hillsides. These were open spaces enclosed by a wall; they had no doors, only narrow openings that allowed sheep to go in and out. To channel the movement of the sheep, the shepherd would lie across the threshold and even sleep there. Thus, the shepherd would literally become the door—no one and nothing went in or out except through (over) the shepherd!

This is a remarkable image of Jesus. As the door, Jesus determines who is invited into community with him and who receives salvation and eternal life. He is the door to a new relationship with God. Through Jesus, Christians find access to God. His door leads to safety and security.

This understanding of Jesus as door must be read against the backdrop of his debate with "the Pharisees" in chapter 9. Jesus had healed a man blind from birth. This healing took place on the Sabbath. (Do you see a pattern developing here?)

This healing is another blot on Jesus' record, according to the religious establishment. Confrontation is inevitable.

Jesus reveals himself as the door for the sheep. No Christian can enter or exit except through him. Those who come before Jesus (verse 8) are those who oppose him, and not all the prophets and saints of the faith. The Pharisees in chapter 9 dismiss Jesus and his works; these are the thieves and bandits. Jesus' opponents seek to kill him and the healed man! They seek to take away life while Jesus gives life!

Jesus is the "door" for the sheep. He must have a flock to follow and depend on him. This implies community. Too often, Christians concentrate on their personal relationship with Jesus and exclude others. Jesus says here that community is essential to well-being and salvation. We who claim Jesus as the good shepherd do so as part of a flock, all with equal status. We hear Jesus' voice, and we follow him—all the way to God! There, in that fellowship, we find abundant life. We are the church because Jesus is (*ego eimi*). Jesus is the door for the sheep; this is an inclusive flock. There is love for all, and each must choose. Again, Jesus invites all, but every person must decide.

We have many doors from which to choose. There are doors that hide known and unknown dangers. There are doors that are pretty to look at but are impenetrable. There are doors that are hollow. Some doors squeak. Some doors do not close properly. Some doors open from the right; others from the left. There are glass doors and wooden doors and steel doors. There are folding doors and sliding doors. There are swinging doors and pocket doors. There are single doors and double doors. We live every day with doors. Most of the time, we do not have to think about them—we open and close them as we will. We are concerned about doors only when they do not function properly—then, they can be a real nuisance. Jesus is the perfect door—this door never malfunctions, never swells in heat and humidity, and never leaks in rain and snow! This door never creaks or bangs in the night. This door holds abundant life—joy, peace, community.

This "I am" saying of Jesus fits John's theology well: right belief in Jesus Christ is rewarded with abundant and eternal life. Jesus is sufficient for all our needs. Jesus is the door that guides us into the abundant life.

MEDITATION

My paternal grandparents operated a family farm in Demopolis. Operating a farm was hard work; they rose with the crow of the rooster, often just before daybreak! They worked hard all day, regardless of the season or the weather. A major concern was the whereabouts of the cows and horses. The farmers often took the animals out to pasture so they could graze and exercise. It was important that the animals be rounded up at the end of the day. They needed to be contained for protection. My grandparents' acres of land were fenced in. On the road leading to my grandparents' house was a barbed wire gate that needed to be opened and closed for traffic—both foot and vehicle. Failure to properly close the gate meant the possibility of the animals getting out, where they could be stolen, lost, or killed.

Even in the rain and the dead of night, someone had to open and close the gate. It seemed like a nuisance until we were reminded that the animals represented a major financial investment. To lose them would mean losing revenue and time. Despite the weather, we dutifully opened and closed the gate.

I imagine Jesus doing the same for us. The gate or door can keep us in or keep us out. It can protect us or reject us. Jesus is the door who lets us decide whether we want in or out. The choice is made by us, and Jesus abides by our choice; we cannot decide for others. We must all decide for ourselves whether we wish to join the community. We, as members of the community, do not have the right to exclude others; only Jesus can do that.

QUESTIONS FOR REFLECTION

1. As the door for the sheep, Jesus provides access to a new life and a new way of being.

   What does an abundant life mean for you?

   What might an abundant life mean for persons in developing countries?

   What doors in your life need opening or closing? Explain.

2. Jesus is the door for the sheep. There are twelve gates (doors) to the city of Jerusalem, signifying that there are many ways to the city of hope and salvation. Both images imply an inclusive position regarding membership. Yet Jesus and the religious establishment were at odds about who was in and who was out.

   How do you reconcile these two images of community?

   Which image does your congregation live out? Explain.

CLOSING PRAYER

Eternal God, we thank you for your abiding presence. You ward off danger even before we are aware of it. In Jesus you have made a way for us to know and love you. For his sacrifice, we are thankful. We are glad that Jesus brings us all together, regardless of those things we think should separate us from one another. We offer this prayer in the name of the one who is the door to you. Amen.

THE GOOD SHEPHERD

Bible Study
"I am the good shepherd."

Read John *10:11–21*

"I am the good shepherd. The good shepherd lays down his life for the sheep."   *(John 10:11)*

Begin with prayer

❦

OVERVIEW

THIS "I AM" saying is a continuation of a discourse started at the end of the ninth chapter. This section concludes Jesus' last public ministry discourse. His self-disclosure now shifts from the door for the sheep to the good shepherd.

The biblical writer highlights the contrast between the good shepherd and the hired hand. Jesus uses the positive image of the shepherd developed in the Hebrew Scriptures. God is seen as an early shepherd of Israel, and the shepherd's duties are most evident in Psalm 23:

> God is my shepherd, I shall not want.
>   God makes me lie down in green pastures;
> God leads me beside still waters;
>   God restores my soul.
> God leads me in right paths
>   for God's name's sake.
>
> Even though I walk through the shadowy valley,
>   I fear no evil;
> for you are with me;

> your rod and your staff—
> they comfort me.
>
> You prepare a table before me
>   in the presence of my enemies;
> you anoint my head with oil;
>   my cup overflows.
> Surely goodness and mercy shall follow me
>   all the days of my life,
> and I shall dwell in the house of God
>   my whole life long.

The good shepherd leads, guides, feeds, protects, and even carries the sheep, when necessary. God cares for the sheep and has their best interests at heart.

There are bad shepherds, too. Jeremiah makes clear that unfaithful shepherds needed to be replaced. God will establish a shepherd who will gather the sheep:

- "I will give you shepherds after my own heart, who will feed you with knowledge and understanding" (Jer. 3:15).
- "I will raise up shepherds over them who will shepherd them, and they shall not fear any longer, or be dismayed, nor shall any be missing, says God" (Jer. 23:4).
- "I will set up over them one shepherd, my servant David, and he shall feed them: he shall feed them and be their shepherd. And I . . . will be their God, and my servant David shall be prince among them; I, God, have spoken" (Ezek. 34:23–24).

Later in Israel's development, some shepherds were thieves and cheats; their roaming lives allowed them to steal the flock. Despite the bad ones, God is still called Israel's Shepherd. God has led the flock out of Egypt, guided it in the present, and will gather it again. In the Hebrew Scriptures, leaders and teachers are called faithful shepherds, on the order of Moses and David.

In the New Testament, shepherds are not cast in a negative light. They know their sheep, seek lost ones, and risk their lives for the flock. Hired hands, however, are cast with thieves and bandits as false shepherds. They have no personal stake in the well-being of the sheep and are concerned only with providing the bare minimum in caring for the sheep. Hired hands do not risk their lives for the sheep although wolves and other wild animals were real threats to the flock:

- "See, I am sending you out like sheep into the midst of wolves; so be wise as serpents and innocent as doves" (Matt. 10:16).
- "I know that after I have gone, savage wolves will come in among you, not sparing the flock" (Acts 20:29).

The good shepherd goes beyond the job out of love for the sheep. The Greek word translated "good" (*kalos*) carries the sense of being ordered, sound, competent, faithful, and praiseworthy. Jesus is the Good Shepherd because of the relationship to the sheep and to God. By claiming to be the Good Shepherd, Jesus fulfills God's promise to Israel given in Ezekiel 34. Jesus' life for the sheep is an act of obedience to God. There is nothing the Good Shepherd would not do for the well-being of the sheep; no sacrifice is too great. Jesus loves God so much that the only desire is to do God's work—even if it means giving up his life.

Further, Jesus gathers the flock. Jesus implies that the community he is forming will be inclusive: "I have other sheep that do not belong to this fold. I must bring them also, and they will listen to my voice. So there will be one flock, one shepherd" (John 10:16). Remember that membership in Jesus' community, according to John, is based on belief and faith. All who *see* Jesus, all who *hear* Jesus, all who *believe in* Jesus are invited in! In Jesus' day, this would have included sinners, lepers, women, Samaritans, tax collectors, and more. As the Good Shepherd, Jesus embodies the powers and functions of Israel's God. Jesus is concerned for individual welfare (he knows each by name) and for communal destiny (he grants the community abundant life). Jesus' sheepfold is open and inclusive.

Every shepherd needs a flock. Interestingly, the image of the sheep is not very flattering. Throughout the Scriptures, sheep are portrayed as stupid creatures. They are not able to take care of themselves and need constant watching. They wander off; they will drink polluted water; they will try to scratch out food from the same barren spot even when fresh grass is right in front of their faces; they will eat too much; and they will fall down and be unable to get up on their own! The sheep are totally dependent creatures. They need a shepherd to guide, care for, and rescue them. Sheep will not survive without a shepherd.

These images go against the grain of who we think we are. We, as a society, applaud those who achieve. We value type A personalities who use their drive, creativity, and energy to achieve success. We emphasize the importance of effective leadership skills and look askance at those who are unwilling or unable to reach their full potential. Bookstore shelves have whole sections devoted to leadership development and self-help books. We want to be all that we can be, and we seek to do all this on our own terms. Our rugged individualism is seen as an asset—we can achieve whatever we set out to do. Initiative is a prerequisite for success.

Given our modern reality, we have difficulty thinking of ourselves as sheep. We would rather be shepherds—in charge and running the show. We like others to be dependent on us; we feel better taking care of others than having others care for us. At the same time, Jesus offers something we desperately long for—to be known! Jesus knows the sheep—and knows us. This relationship mirrors the relationship between Jesus and God.

We long to be known and understood. It is a great human need. Getting to know a person is a difficult, long-term proposition. We dole out parts of ourselves in stingy bits and pieces. We do not want to risk being vulnerable with one another. We do not mean to hold back, we just cannot seem to help ourselves. We judge one another cruelly and by impossible standards. Our well-intentioned actions are misunderstood. Our overtures are rejected. We avoid commitments because we think we will be abused or exploited. We have a hard time trusting one another.

Jesus tells us that our anxiety and emptiness can be relieved if we place our trust in him and depend on him. We can trust him because he is willing to die for us. What an incredible gesture! And all are invited to join the flock.

Jesus relates to *the flock*. He knows each individual sheep by name; he cares for each one, but he relates to the group. The community of faith, the flock, receives abundant life because of its relationship to Jesus. The flock is his own. If we extend the metaphor of Jesus as the Good Shepherd, we then are his flock. We can wholly trust in and depend on him. As his flock, we have certain responsibilities to fulfill. Our individual and collective lives need to reflect the life of our shepherd—caring for the rest of the flock and all of creation. This does not mean that some are better than others, but rather it means that we love one another as Jesus loves us. The fate of the sheep depends on the character of the shepherd. The flock flourishes or perishes because of the shepherd. Jesus tells us that his flock has abundant life because of who he is and what he does on

our behalf. Jesus provides ultimate care, guidance, and protection.

This is a powerful image for John's outcast community. The
Christians were cut off from their Jewish foundations, but they
had found a new home in Jesus, the Good Shepherd. Rather
than live smugly in that knowledge and assurance, they saw
Jesus as the one who gathers other outcasts and gives them all
abundant life. The only thing they had to do was truly *see* Jesus
and believe in him as God's Messiah. It should not shock us to
know that many did believe—but some still refused to believe
in Jesus.

MEDITATION

My first visit to the Middle East in 1992 was jarring. Our tour
group left New York City's Kennedy Airport, and we were warned
that security would be tight. When we changed planes in Lon-
don, we experienced "real" security. My checked luggage was
pulled from the plane, and I was asked to accompany a female
security guard to a small room. I unlocked all my bags and
watched her empty my suitcases and search through my be-
longings. She had me repack each of the three bags. I was then
body-searched. Finally, one hour later, I was cleared to board
the flight to Tel Aviv. (It pays always to arrive at the airport early!)
Upon our arrival in Tel Aviv, once again a great deal of time
passed before we were permitted to board the bus to the West
Bank. We were questioned, individually and in small clusters.
One member of our group was escorted to a small room to be
interrogated before she was cleared to enter the country.

I was struck by the number of young women and men wield-
ing automatic weapons. They were Israeli soldiers who had or-
ders to shoot first and ask questions later. We were admonished
to keep our passports with us at all times and not to wander off

alone. We were aware that our visit to the Middle East carried the risk of witnessing or experiencing violence. We knew we were being watched all the time. Every visit to Jerusalem, the Holy City, was observed by Israeli troops who sat along the wall surrounding the city. Our inquiries for directions or assistance were met with outright hostility; we never felt fully comfortable or relaxed. The land that produced three major world religions—Judaism, Islam, and Christianity—was a land at war with itself and with the rest of the world. We were in a strange land, and we knew it!

In contrast to the military presence, the land itself held a special appeal. We visited Bethany, Bethlehem, Jericho, and Nazareth. We walked up the mountain to Masada. We stood in the waters of the Dead Sea and the Jordan River. We walked in the Garden of Gethsemane and wandered through the various quarters of Jerusalem. We gazed upon the city from the rooftops of Jerusalem homes. We traveled the rugged hills and tasted the dust of the treacherous roads. We walked where Jesus walked, and we baked under the heat of the Palestinian sun. We traveled miles, marveling at the arid desert and the incredible oases that sprang up out of nowhere. In the middle of brown sand stood stately palm trees with streams of water at their bases.

And we saw shepherds and their flocks! I was startled to see the number of female shepherds, having always pictured shepherds as strong men who can lift sheep caught in the brush. I was pleasantly surprised to learn that God also calls women to be shepherds. This realization expanded my view of vocation and calling. Contrary to what the patriarchal worldview would have us believe, God's plans for abundant life include women as vessels and instruments of God's work! If Jesus is the Good Shepherd, both men and women can be under-shepherds—thanks be to God!

QUESTIONS FOR REFLECTION

1. How are human beings like sheep?
2. What does it mean to live as one of Jesus' sheep? How do you know when Jesus is calling you?
3. What does a church that defines itself as the flock of Jesus look like? How does it function in its community? How does it present itself to the world?
4. When we consider this passage of Scripture, we tend to identify with the Good Shepherd. In what ways are we like thieves and bandits? In what ways are we like hired hands? What are the implications of these images for church leadership?
5. Flocks are threatened by internal and external dangers. What dangers do you face as a member of Jesus' flock?
6. What dangers does your church face as Jesus' flock?

CLOSING PRAYER

Eternal God, we thank you for your loving-kindness. We thank you for the gift of Jesus, who is our Good Shepherd. Open our hearts and minds to receive this gift. Open our eyes and ears so we will see Jesus and hear when we are called. Move us, O God, to respond willingly and joyfully. We pray in the name of the Christ, who knows us by name. Amen.

THE RESURRECTION AND THE LIFE

Bible Study
"I am the resurrection and the life."

Read John 11:17–27

Jesus said to her, "I am the resurrection and the life. Those who believe in me, even though they die, will live, and everyone who lives and believes in me will never die. Do you believe this?" (*John 11:25–26*)

Begin with prayer

⬤

OVERVIEW

CHAPTER 11 CONTAINS THE last sign of Jesus' public ministry. The resurrection of Lazarus occurs only in John's Gospel. The act of raising Lazarus leads directly to Jesus' death. This story is taut and suspenseful, conveying the drama that accompanied Jesus throughout his ministry.

Lazarus, Mary, and Martha were great friends of Jesus. When Lazarus becomes ill, the sisters are convinced that Jesus can make him well. Jesus has healed strangers; surely he will take care of his good friend. The sisters send a message to Jesus, who does not act right away. After two days, Jesus tells his disciples that he has decided to visit Lazarus. Jesus is a wanted man in Judea; "the Jews" are looking to kill him. But Jesus insists that they go: the work of God must be done while the opportunity exists. Then he states that his task is not to avoid "the Jews" but to awaken Lazarus.

Again, there is a misunderstanding. The disciples are not willing to risk their lives to serve as Lazarus's alarm clock. Jesus states plainly, then, that Lazarus is dead. Jesus will work a miracle so that God will be glorified.

Jesus and the disciples journey to Bethany, only about two miles from Jerusalem where "the Jews" were waiting to arrest Jesus. This note of geography heightens the drama: certain death is just a little way off. Despite the danger, Jesus decides when to go to Bethany and, by implication, makes a decision about when he will die.

Lazarus has been dead for four days—this is an important element of the story. According to the popular view of the time, the soul of a dead person hovers over the body in an attempt to reenter it. After three days, the soul leaves the body forever. After four days, Lazarus is really dead! The mourning continues, according to the custom. Friends and neighbors are expected to join the mourning family in its grief, which is marked by animated and loud weeping and wailing.

Martha leaves the mourning and runs out to meet Jesus on the road. In her pain and disappointment that Jesus has not come in time to save her brother, she makes the accusation that "if you had been here, my brother would not have died." She believes that Jesus' delay has prevented her brother's recuperation. While she accuses Jesus of neglect, she hopes that something can yet be done, affirming, "But even now, I know that God will give you whatever you ask of him." Curiously, Martha does not tell Jesus what she wants—she leaves the matter in his hands.

Jesus offers words of comfort that she will see her brother again. Martha responds with the prevailing belief of her time that there will be a general resurrection on the last day. In early Israel, there was no belief in a life after death: "The dead do not praise God, nor do any that go down into silence" (Ps. 115:17). The Israelites believed that the soul went to Sheol, the underworld where departed souls go. While both good and evil souls went to Sheol, there is no biblical evidence that it was a place of torture.

As the nation evolved, the belief developed in a general resurrection of the dead:

- "Your dead shall live, their corpses shall rise. O dwellers in the dust, awake and sing for joy! For your dew is a radiant dew, and the earth will give birth to those long dead" (Isa. 26:19).
- "Many of those who sleep in the dust of the earth shall awake, some to everlasting life, and some to shame and everlasting contempt" (Dan. 12:2).

Resurrection meant a complex and total change of the human being. Those resurrected would shine like stars (see Dan. 12:3) or be like angels (see Mark 12:25). Resurrection was seen as a communal event—God would raise up all of God's people.

In Jesus' day, the Sadducees did not believe in an afterlife:

When Paul noticed that some were Sadducees and others were Pharisees, he called out in the council, "Brothers, I am a Pharisee, a son of Pharisees. I am on trial concerning the hope of the resurrection of the dead." When he said this, a dissension began between the Pharisees and the Sadducees, and the assembly was divided. (The Sadducees say that there is no resurrection, or angel, or spirit; but the Pharisees acknowledge all three.) (Acts 23:6–8)

Jesus declares, "I am the resurrection and the life." The promise of the resurrection is fulfilled in Jesus. Jesus is both resurrection and life; Jesus controls the believer's present life and the life to come. As the resurrection, Jesus has power over death; physical death, therefore, is not ultimate. As the life, Jesus pro-

vides life beyond death; Jesus is the final reality, not death.
Glimpses of this hope are seen in the Hebrew Scriptures:

> Therefore my heart is glad, and
>   my soul rejoices;
>   my body also rests secure.
> For you do not give me up to
>   Sheol,
> or let your faithful one see the Pit.
>
> You show me the path of life.
>   In your presence there is fullness of joy;
>   in your right hand are pleasures forevermore.
>
> (Ps. 16:9–11)

One of the fullest expressions of Jesus as resurrection and the
life is seen in Romans 8:35–39:

Who will separate us from the love of Christ? Will hardship,
or distress, or persecution, or famine, or nakedness, or peril,
or sword? As it is written,

> "For your sake we are being killed
>   all day long;
> we are accounted as sheep to be
>   slaughtered."

No, in all these things we are more than conquerors through
him who loved us. For I am convinced that neither death, nor
life, nor angels, nor rulers, nor things present, nor things to
come, nor powers, nor height, nor depth, nor anything else in
all creation, will be able to separate us from the love of God in
Christ Jesus.

The expectation of the future is behind Jesus' self-disclosure as the resurrection and the life.

Jesus continues his self-revelation: those who believe in him will live despite physical death. Again, those who live and believe in Jesus will never die. Jesus is the ultimate answer, not death. Jesus opens the way for an eternal relationship with God for all who believe.

Jesus then asks Martha an important question: "Do you believe this?" Her confession of faith parallels that of Peter in Matthew 16:16 ("You are the Messiah, the Child of the Living God"). Martha says, "Yes, . . . I believe that you are the Messiah, the Child of God, the one coming into the world." This is *the* statement of faith. The rest of the story seems almost anticlimactic.

Martha goes back to the house to tell Mary that Jesus is asking for her. Mary reacts in the same way as Martha does. However, as Mary kneels down before Jesus, she accuses him of neglect, too. She does so in the presence of the mourners who are accompanying her on the road.

Jesus reacts intensely. The translation of the Greek in verse 33, "he was greatly disturbed in spirit and deeply moved," does not fully convey the meaning. The verb *embrimaomai* implies indignation; its root means "to snort with anger." The second verb, *tarasso*, implies agitation or being stirred up. The New Revised Standard Version softens the language so that we see Jesus' pity, love, and compassion rather than his indignation and anger. We are left wondering why Jesus was so upset: Was he angry because of the sisters' complaint? Was he angry because death had claimed his good friend? Was he angry because he did not see his friend before he died? Was he angry because the crowd intruded on his time with his friends? Was he angry because his own death was imminent? We simply do not know, and scholars are undecided.

What we do know is that Jesus was upset. And we know that he wept! Jesus publicly displayed the pain of death that we all experience. The response of the crowd of mourners is divided: some see the display as evidence of Jesus' love for Lazarus; others continue the sisters' complaint that Jesus has not saved Lazarus from death.

Jesus' claim as the resurrection and the life is powerful; in him is God's power over death. Because Jesus and God are one, we can live freely and die calmly. Both life and death are in God's hands—this is a blessed assurance for all who believe. Who Jesus is, along with what he does, mark a new world order. There is nothing to separate us from God, not even death. We can live and die in joy because we know everything will be okay. We need not live any longer in fear because Jesus is the resurrection and the life, and "God did not give us a spirit of cowardice, but rather a spirit of power and of love and of self-discipline" (2 Tim. 1:7).

This miracle of Lazarus's new life is troublesome to modern readers. We ponder whether this event actually happened. We want proof, because our experience teaches us that resurrection is scientifically impossible. Once a body dies, it stays dead. We question the validity of this miracle as well as all the others that Jesus performed. We want to know if the resurrection happened and how, then we want to know whether it can happen again. Popular culture feeds into this through science fiction literature and movies. A part of us wants to believe in resurrection despite all that we know about death.

Ultimately, we are left to wonder. Belief in Jesus and his works relies on faith, not fact. This is not to dismiss our questions and doubt. Rather, it is to acknowledge the mystery of our faith. We will never know enough about God, Jesus Christ, or the Holy Spirit to prove their existence and presence. We do not know and will never know whether an actual dead man named Lazarus was physically raised to life again. We cannot prove the facts of this act of Jesus.

All we know is that something remarkable happened and continues to happen when women and men, girls and boys encounter Jesus. Those who see and hear experience something beyond the ability to prove that such experiences are real—we just know what we know. This is what mystery is about: simply knowing what we know. Our faith is not in creeds or doctrines; our faith rests upon the relationship of Jesus with the God who has granted Jesus a share of God's power. Jesus loves us, and we are different because of that love. We have known Jesus as bread and light. We have known Jesus as door and good shepherd. What keeps us from now knowing Jesus as resurrection and life?

MEDITATION

Jesus as the resurrection and the life amazes us. Jesus brings life out of death, and we wish we could do that. But only Jesus, working for God, brings forth life. We, however, are not passive bystanders.

When Jesus reached the tomb of Lazarus, he gave instructions to those gathered. His instructions apply to us as well: "Take away the stone."

There are a multitude of stones to be moved. Within ourselves, there are stones to be moved: selfishness, insensitivity, dishonesty, apathy. We know that we are not perfect. We try our best to be good people. We live in tombs that stink with the horrors of shame, guilt, and despair. We do not choose to live in these tombs, but sin and its seductiveness make us dead inside. Jesus asks us to move the stones so that we can hear his voice, which brings healing and new life. Jesus calls each of us by name. As we come forth when beckoned, Jesus gives us health and healing.

When we survey this nation, we see tombs of death:

- There are those who are homeless and scramble nightly for sleeping space in subway stations and public parks.
- There are those who are hungry and huddle around signs that say, "Will work for food."
- There are those who are addicted to crack and cocaine, and risk life and limb for bigger and better highs.
- There are those who become parents much too young—before they even know who they are or what they can become.
- There are those who live under the threat of bodily harm: homosexuals, Jews, people of color.

To these and other tombs of fear and devastation, Jesus commands us to move the stones:

- The problems of this world are massive and overwhelming. We are helpless, so Jesus tells us to move the stones.
- The evils of this world are the result of unjust systems, powers, and principalities. We are powerless, so Jesus tells us to move the stones.
- The demons we fight within ourselves are pervasive and seductive. We are weak, so Jesus tells us to move the stones.

We are told to move the stones so Jesus can go to work. Jesus tells us to do what we can and as much as we can, then get out of the way! We are told to do the best we can, then leave the rest to Jesus. Jesus tells us to have faith and trust because Jesus and God have all power—the power of the resurrection and the power of the life. Do you believe this?

QUESTIONS FOR REFLECTION

1. What in your personal life needs resurrection and new life? Explain.
2. What in your congregation and/or community needs resurrection? How might you roll away the stones that block the miracle of new life in those places?
3. Do you fear death? How might the preaching and teaching of the church help persons live well and die well?
4. How do you react to Jesus' anger and agitation in this week's biblical passage? What is the impact of such knowledge on your faith?
5. Life has a rhythm of dying and rising, winter and spring. How does your spiritual life reflect these rhythms? Does the church year help or hinder your rhythm?

CLOSING PRAYER

Eternal God, we are gathered in your presence, and we thank you for this grace. You stand at the tombs of our being, asking us to choose between life and death, blessing and curse. We choose life. O God, help us to live freely and joyously. Then, when it is our time, help us to die in peace. We pray in the name of the one who calls us by name. Amen.

THE WAY, THE TRUTH, AND THE LIFE

Bible Study
"I am the way, and the truth, and the life."

Read John *13:31–14:11*

Jesus said to him, "I am the way, and the truth, and the life.
No one comes to the Father except through me."

(John 14:6)

Begin with prayer

⊱✦⊰

OVERVIEW

THIS "I AM" SAYING OF JESUS is addressed to his disciples after
their departure from Bethany. After Jesus raises Lazarus, some
of the crowd believe in Jesus and others go to tattle to the
religious officials in Jerusalem. The chief priests and Pharisees decide to kill Jesus, reasoning that it is better for one man
to die than to jeopardize the Holy City and the nation. They
are afraid that they will be persecuted by the Roman govern-
ment for Jesus' popularity.

Jesus and his disciples go to Ephraim to hide out. About a
week before the Passover, Jesus goes back to Bethany to see
Lazarus, Martha, and Mary, who hold a dinner in his honor.
Mary anoints Jesus' feet with costly perfumed oil. Jesus chas-
tises Judas, who protests what he perceives to be a waste of
good money. The crowd hears of Jesus' visit, and they come to
see Jesus and Lazarus, the man raised from the dead. The chief
priests plan to kill Jesus and Lazarus.

The next day, the crowd hears that Jesus is going to Jerusalem. Jesus' entry into the Holy City is marked by great celebration by those who believe in him. They claim him as their ruler:

So they took branches of palm trees and went out to meet him, shouting,

> "Hosanna!
> Blessed is the one who comes in
> the name of God—
> the Ruler of Israel!" (John 12:13)

The chief priests and religious officials are convinced that their plan to kill Jesus is correct. He has won over the people, and that is a dangerous thing.

Jesus engages in a lengthy conversation with his disciples, some visiting Greeks, and the crowd—he talks about his death as necessary and life-giving. John reminds us of a recurring theme—some believe Jesus because of his self-revelation and his good works. Some still refuse to believe that Jesus is the Messiah (see John 12:44–50). The scene shifts to a private meal which Jesus shares with his disciples.

This "I am" saying is pronounced after the foot-washing ceremony (John 13:1–11). Jesus talks about the joy of servant ministry (John 13:12–20) and predicts Judas's betrayal (John 13:21–30). Jesus commands the disciples to love one another (John 13:31–38). The disciples are sad and scared.

It is against the backdrop of intimacy, resignation, and overwhelming sorrow that Jesus speaks these words: "I am the way, and the truth, and the life. No one comes to God except through me." Jesus tries to prepare his disciples for the course of events about to happen: his arrest, trial, crucifixion, and resurrection.

Jesus begins with words of comfort and assurance. He challenges them to stay strong in the midst of the tragedy that awaits them. Jesus tells them to rely on their faith, to believe in him, and that their faith will see them through.

Jesus' "Father's house" may mean heaven; but, as we have seen earlier, location is also symbolic of relationship. Jesus tells us where he is from (above) so that we can understand the relationship to God (as child). Therefore, in this intimate relationship, there are many "dwelling places." The Greek noun *mone* is from a verb meaning "to dwell, abide, or stay." The word appears in only two places in the New Testament: John 14:2 and John 14:23! Here, the word emphasizes that Jesus has prepared a place for all believers to stay in God's house. Because of Jesus' relationship with God and with us, we have an eternal home with God and will never be homeless. In John 14:23, God's house is here on earth; God and Jesus will come to believers and make their home with them. These images go back to the Hebrew Scriptures:

- "And have them make me a sanctuary, so that I may dwell among them" (Exod. 25:8).
- "I will make a covenant of peace with them; it shall be an everlasting covenant with them; and I will bless them and multiply them, and will set my sanctuary among them forevermore. My dwelling place shall be with them; and I will be their God, and they shall be my people" (Ezek. 37:26–27).

In John, salvation is union with God and Jesus, and this bond is indestructible and eternal. Jesus' return is the assurance and promise that he is the resurrection and life; death will not sever the relationship between Jesus and his believers. The disciples have a place in God's house as full members of the household. They enter the door as friends, not as servants (see John 13:16–17).

Jesus declares he is the "way" (Greek: *hodos*). This word appears nearly nine hundred times in the Greek version of the Hebrew Scriptures; it most often means a literal path or road. Life, itself, is called a "way," a journey. The word also means a manner of life or behavior. Israel talked a lot about the ways

of God and the ways in which God's people should conduct
themselves:

- "You must therefore be careful to do as . . . God has
  commanded you; you shall not turn to the right or to the
  left. You must follow exactly the path that . . . God has
  commanded you, so that you may live, and that it may go
  well with you, and that you may live long in the land that
  you are to possess" (Deut. 5:32–33).
- "Teach me your way, O God, and lead me on a level path
  because of my enemies" (Ps. 27:11).
- "And when you turn to the right or when you turn to the
  left, your ears shall hear a word behind you, saying, 'This
  is the way; walk in it'" (Isa. 30:21).
- "Thus says God, your Redeemer, the Holy One of Israel: 'I
  am your . . . God, who teaches you for your own good,
  who leads you in the way you should go'" (Isa. 48:17).

Language of "the way" was familiar to the original hearers of
John's Gospel. Jesus is the embodiment of God's way. If the
believer desires to be with God, look to Jesus! If the believer
desires to live with God, look to Jesus!

Further, Jesus is the "truth" (Greek: *aletheia*). This word is
common in the Hebrew Scriptures:

> Teach me your way, O God,
>> that I may walk in your truth;
> give me an undivided heart to
>> revere your name. (Ps. 86:11)

The word denotes authenticity. Some people will tell the truth,
but Jesus is its embodiment. To know Jesus is to know the truth.
Jesus makes the truth of God available to believers.

Lastly, Jesus is the "life" (Greek: *zoe*). In the Hebrew Scriptures, life is the ultimate good. Life is more than physical existence; it includes vitality, purpose, meaning, and direction. Life itself is a gift from God, and God is the source of all life:

- When you hide your face, they are
     dismayed;
   when you take away their
      breath, they die
   and return to their dust.
   When you send forth your spirit,
      they are created;
   and you renew the face of the
      ground. (Ps. 104:29–30)

- For what will it profit them to gain the whole world and forfeit their life? Indeed, what can they give in return for their life? (Mark 8:36–37)

Jesus is life because he is God's creative, life-giving power. Those who believe in Jesus have eternal life—the body may die, but the soul is not destroyed. It lives with God in God's house. Believers have life because they are committed to Christ.

The disciples do not understand what Jesus is saying; will they ever learn? Jesus is exasperated but continues his explanation, which should be crystal clear by now: Jesus and God are one!

Throughout his public ministry, Jesus invited persons to follow him. He was saying, in essence, that his followers should do as he did and not just as he said. Jesus does not *tell* us the way, he is the way! Following Jesus means walking in a new quality of life and finding a new way of being. There are other paths that beckon—the way of success and achievement, the way of rugged individualism. You can add to the list! But the way to real life, to abundant life, is Jesus!

The most troubling part of this week's passage is the second part of verse 6: "No one comes to the Father except through me." For John, these words expressed his belief that Jesus, God's Word made flesh, fundamentally changed the relationship between God and humanity. Jesus is the embodiment of God's presence here and now. "The Father" can only be known through Jesus. When we encounter and experience Jesus, we encounter and experience God. Thereby, we know God because of Jesus.

John's conviction, however, has been used as a weapon by some Christians to denigrate persons of other faith convictions. At this point, Gail R. O'Day's commentary on John in *The New Interpreter's Bible* is helpful. In summary, her argument is:

- John's claim is that of a community that understands itself to be in relationship to God through the incarnation of Jesus Christ. This God is known to them as "Father" or "Parent."
- John 14:6b is the particular confession of a particular community about a specific event. Jesus is the tangible presence of God's love for the world. God is the specific one who is known in the life and death of Jesus of Nazareth. Jesus' words "no one" mean "none of you."

It is important to remember that John's community has been cut off from its Jewish roots and traditions. The Judaic God was distant and remote. The Christ, God's Messiah, has appeared in human form and has shared our common lot. This is miraculous and mysterious. John does not claim that his faith community is a world religion; his is the conviction of a persecuted, rejected religious minority. This minority has established a new "home" grounded in the reality that God's Word became flesh; of this the community is sure, and on this they will stake their lives.

O'Day concludes that John expresses his understanding and experience of God, and those who would join this community must claim as he does: God's love is seen in the coming of Jesus. John does not deny that there are other ways to God. Rather, he is calling those who will hear to listen to Jesus, who comes from God. John has made clear that anyone who sees Jesus has seen God. Anyone who hears Jesus has heard God. Anyone who believes in Jesus has believed in God.

It is extremely important that we do not use John's convictions to make ourselves feel superior on the world stage. John's words are not the final judge on how others understand and experience God. John's Gospel is not concerned with other religions of his day and region. Nor is it concerned with bringing Jews, Taoists, Muslims, Hindus, or New Age adherents to Jesus. John's is a celebratory confession of faith for a particular group of early followers of Jesus, who are rooted and grounded and centered in the incarnation of God's Word. John's main concern is to make clear what his community believes and why; it is not to convince the world that Christianity is the supreme religion.

This point cannot be overstated. Once we understand John's intentions and lift our modern insecurities from the text, we, too, can celebrate with John. For Christians, Jesus is the way to God. We cannot get to God unless we believe that Jesus is God's Christ.

If the Christian life is a journey, then Jesus is the route *and* the reason for the journey. For us, Jesus is the only way to God. For Christians, Jesus is the way, and the truth, and the life; in him, all three come together and all three point to God!

MEDITATION

The opening verses of chapter 14 are most often used for funerals and memorial services. The church teaches about death and resurrection at funerals or during the Easter season. It is important to teach and preach about death during the daily and seasonal rhythms of life. The occasion of a funeral, when a family needs pastoral care over the loss of a loved one, is not the time to reflect on one's life in view of Jesus' resurrection and the new life that brings.

We need to see the power of the resurrection in our everyday lives because we live each day in the face of death. We speak of being in the land of the living ("I believe that I shall see the goodness of God in the land of the living" [Ps. 27:13]); but we are dying from the moment we are born. We are challenged to integrate death into the church's theological reflection and pastoral-care teachings for the purpose of helping our members overcome their fear of death and to claim God's promises of life, both now and forever.

A possible way of doing this might look like my meditation below.

Home

"Let not your hearts be troubled." Recognizing the love and care in these words, preachers have used this passage to reassure us that death is not the final answer. It reminds us that we are on a journey to God's house—the house with many rooms. The term "dwelling places" conveys space to stretch out and places to be who we are. Some of us currently live in cramped, narrow, small places. We are pushed into corners that are stuffy and uncomfortable. In God's house, however, we have an image of an expansive place—with room for all to come and find adequate space. We are left with the impression that we can go to God's house just as we are. We are left with the impression that God is anxiously awaiting our arrival.

As a child, I was always excited when out-of-town guests came to visit. My mother would rally us kids and delegate duties: there were floors to be mopped and waxed; there were curtains to be washed, starched, and ironed; there were sheets to be washed, bleached, and ironed; there was furniture to be polished and bathrooms to be disinfected. If someone truly special was expected, the preparations included having things they really liked: Big Mama liked lemon cake; Aunt Nell always wanted an extra quilt, even in the summertime; Uncle Dee liked a radio on his nightstand; Mama Dora liked a Bible next to her bed. The special touches were for special people; we knew them, and we knew what they liked. We wanted each person to feel at home. Our guests were encouraged to not worry, to relax, and to make themselves at home.

Wouldn't it be wonderful if we believed God did the same for us? Would we be less terrified of death and dying if we thought someone was expecting us? Would we talk more about how we want to die if we thought someone was preparing a place for us?

I know that death and dying are hard topics to talk about. But they are even harder to go through. I have had a lot of encounters with death. My maternal grandmother and my younger brother both died on the same day in January 1978. Dealing with the deaths of two of my favorite people was the first real test of my faith. For hours, I was chilled and numb. I could not remember any Bible verses; I was at a loss for words to even pray. All I could do was mumble, "Lord, have mercy. Lord, have mercy." I did not even realize what I was saying; I thought the pain would never end; I thought the tears would never stop. But at some point, I don't know when, I started to feel a peace and a calm I had not known. The knot in my stomach loosened. The tension in my shoulders and arms decreased.

Suddenly, I knew, without knowing how I knew, that mercy had arrived. Suddenly, I knew, without knowing how I knew, that my grandmother and brother were fine. It was as if they sent angels to calm me and reassure me that I was not alone.

I never got over their dying, but I am able to remember them with joy. The tears flow from time to time, and I do not try to stop them. And every time I cry, I also remember some funny incident I shared with each of them. Mixed in with my tears is laughter. My sadness is balanced by the joy I shared with them. Somehow, I got through the grief and sorrow.

It was this knowledge that enabled me to get through the illnesses and deaths of other loved ones, including my father and mother, who died a year apart in 1984 and 1985, respectively. There was no way I could prepare for my father's death, even after his long illness. Certainly, I was not prepared for my mother's sudden death. Yet somehow, I made it through. I mourned and my grief was intense and real. Had I had any pride, I would have been embarrassed—but this time I knew, and knew that I knew, that everything would be all right. I knew because God had already carried me through the valley of the shadow of death. I knew because we managed to talk about death in our family before it happened. When my father said to me, "I know the Lord, and I am not afraid to die," I knew I could let him go. He was ready, and I would get ready. He knew he was going home, and he was ready. Although my mother died unexpectedly and quickly, she, too, was ready to go home. I imagine my grandmother and brother and father waiting for her, excited about having her in their midst.

Well, this is not a morbid sharing of my trials. This is a celebration of the mercy and grace, the peace and joy that Jesus brings to us who believe. Jesus knows the pain of loss; he wept at the tomb of Lazarus. Jesus knew the loneliness of loss; he cried from the cross, "My God! My God! Why have you forsaken me?" Jesus knew the peace of going home: "Father, into your hands I commend my spirit." Jesus is the resurrection and the life; Jesus is the way, the truth, and the life. His journey on earth was so human; his purpose was to show us a new way of living and a new way of dying. Whether we live or whether we die, we are God's, and that makes everything all right!

"Let not your hearts be troubled. Believe in God, believe also in me. In God's house there are many dwelling places. I go to prepare a place for you. Where I am, there you may be also. I am the way and the truth and the life." I imagine that Jesus is waiting for us to come home.

While we are living, we must live to the fullest. We must give our best to God and give cheerful service to our sisters and brothers. But when it is time, may we go home with the assurance that Jesus has overcome the power of death and we live in eternal bliss with our Parent and Creator.

Gloria Naylor, in *Mama Day,* has said that we can move away from home, but we never really leave it—not as long as home holds something to be missed!

QUESTIONS FOR REFLECTION

1. When I was about seven years old, my maternal great-grandmother lived in a house on a hill in Demopolis, Alabama. Her daughter, my great-aunt, lived in a house on a neighboring hill. A gravel road connected the two hills. The walk to my great-aunt's house took about thirty minutes. However, these two women often took a shortcut through a swamplike valley between the two hills. The shortcut took about ten minutes. My great-grandmother took me through the shortcut one hot summer day. She flung her ax across her shoulder and told me to follow her. As we entered the woods, she led me on a well-worn path. Inside this forest, the air was cool and the trees were overgrown and uncontrolled. The ground was damp. A

narrow stream ran along the path. I could see huge spider webs and nests hanging from the trees. There were all kinds of noises as birds and wild animals skittered and played. When I looked carefully, I saw fat snakes, black ones and green ones, twined around tree branches. There were all kinds of weird-looking things swimming in the stream. I was really scared, but my great-grandmother grasped my hand and assured me I was safe and that we were almost there. As we emerged from the forest-swamp, a huge black snake slithered across our path. We and the snake stopped. I screamed, and my great-grandmother took her ax and chopped the snake in half. She told me to stop screaming; she had taken care of the danger. For that time and for the rest of her life, she was my way!

Have you had a similar experience of being afraid in unfamiliar surroundings that seemed dangerous? Explain.

How is Jesus the "way" for you?

Have you ever been the "way" for someone else? Explain.

How would you teach this week's scripture passage?

2. If you had to express your personal statement of faith on a bumper sticker, what would it say? Explain.

3. Jesus is the way and the truth and the life. What are the implications of this "I am" saying for church leadership?

CLOSING PRAYER

Eternal God, thank you for making a way out of no way; thank you for being truth in the face of untruth; thank you for being life in the midst of death. As you did in the beginning, let your Spirit hover and brood over us, and in your wisdom, call forth beauty and order from the chaos that pervades our lives. We pray in the name of the one whom you sent to be the way, Christ Jesus! Amen.

THE TRUE VINE

Bible Study
"I am the true vine."

Read John 15:1–17

*"I am the vine, you are the branches. Those who abide in me
and I in them bear much fruit, because apart from me you can
do nothing."*   (*John 15:5*)

Begin with prayer

OVERVIEW

FOR THE PAST SEVEN WEEKS, we have seen Jesus take the ordinary stuff of life and faith and transform it into God's promises fulfilled. He has taken symbols and images already familiar and meaningful to the emerging new community and washed them with his special insight:

- Can we ever see a loaf and not see Jesus as the bread of life, which satisfies our hunger for all time?
- Can we ever see light and not think of Jesus, whose brightness illuminates our dimmest moments?
- Can we ever see a sheepfold and not feel reassured that Jesus is the door that makes available eternal access to our Creator?
- Can we ever hear the soft bleating of sheep and not think of Jesus, the Good Shepherd, who calls us each by name?
- Can we ever watch the devastation of death and not think of Jesus as the resurrection and the life, who calls forth new life and new being?
- Can we ever find ourselves at a crossroads and not consider Jesus, who is the way and the truth and the life?

And so, we come to Jesus' final "I am" saying—Jesus is the true vine. How fitting that Jesus would end his time with his disciples by leaving an image of community and judgment and unspeakable joy.

This final saying continues his concluding discourse with his disciples. Jesus has just given them directions about how to live as a community when he will no longer be with them. They are to keep his commandments as evidence of their love for him. Jesus tells them that God will send another advocate who will comfort and encourage them. Jesus has left his peace with the disciples; he is now ready to be on his way to death.

His parting words are meant to give the disciples strength, because their faith will be sorely tested in the ensuing days. Jesus takes the time to reassure them that everything he is and everything he does is God's work.

Jesus reveals himself in terms familiar to his original audience. Israel had already developed the image of God as vinedresser and itself as vine:

- "You brought a vine out of Egypt, you drove out the nations and planted it" (Ps. 80:8).
- "For the vineyard of the God of hosts is the house of Israel, and the people of Judah are God's pleasant planting; God expected justice, but saw bloodshed; righteousness, but heard a cry!" (Isa. 5:7).
- "Yet I planted you as a choice vine, from the purest stock. How then did you turn degenerate and become a wild vine?" (Jer. 2:21).
- "Israel is a luxuriant vine that yields its fruit. The more Israel's fruit increased the more altars Israel built; as the country improved, Israel improved the pillars" (Hos. 10:1).

Vines, thick trailing plants that attach themselves to other things, were common in Palestine; they required a lot of attention if they were to flourish. Even a casual observer would be struck by the overabundance of vines in the Middle East: they grow thickly on trees, on trellises, on the ground, and on terraces. Vines grow quickly and have to be planted at least twelve feet apart. Even then, they will become overgrown, wild, and unwieldy.

It is impossible to think of vines without thinking of the pruning that they require. In the Middle East, young vines were not allowed to produce fruit for the first few years. This meant a drastic pruning was needed so that the plant would develop to its fullest. Vines, then, would produce two kinds of branches: those that bore fruit and those that did not. Both were needed if a vine was to flourish. Vineyards were a long-term investment. The land had to be prepared—soil cultivated and stones cleared. Many vineyards were surrounded by walls to keep predators out:

> Catch us the foxes,
>   the little foxes,
> that ruin the vineyards—
>   for our vineyards are in blossom.
>   (Song of Sol. 2:15)

The leaves and fruit of the vines are the trademarks of the vine. On the other hand, its woody branches are useless. The softness of the wood made them unfit even for burnt offerings at God's altar:

> O mortal, how does the wood of
>   the vine surpass all
>   other wood—
> the vine branch that is among
>   the trees of the forest?
> Is wood taken from it to make
>   anything?

> Does one take a peg from it on
>   which to hang any object?
> It is put in the fire for fuel;
>   when the fire has consumed
>   both ends of it
> and the middle of it is charred,
>   is it useful for anything?
> When it was whole it was used
>   for nothing;
>   how much less—when the fire
>   has consumed it,
>   and it is charred—
>   can it ever be used for anything!
>   (Ezek. 15:2–5)

The sign of prosperity was a fruitful yield. Persons with vine-yards who had not enjoyed them were excused from serving in the army:

> Has anyone planted a vineyard but not yet enjoyed its fruit?
> He should go back to his house, or he might die in the battle
> and another be first to enjoy its fruit. (Deut. 20:6)

The tragedy of war was symbolized by a damaged vineyard: broken walls, overrun with weeds and thorns, and branches stomped by wild animals. Rebuilding after war and exile would be a time for planting new vineyards: "They shall build houses and inhabit them; they shall plant vineyards and eat their fruit" (Isa. 65:21).

Israel's perspective concerning vines and their fruits was clear: both were gifts from God. The nation saw itself as a vine planted and cared for by God. Jesus' revelation about himself forms a marvelous triangular relationship: God, Jesus, and the community of believers. Each is symbolized by the three elements needed for bountiful harvests: vinedresser, vine, and branches.

In his declaration, Jesus makes clear that he is not God; God is greater than he. God is the source and guide for the work of Jesus, as he has repeated over and over again. Jesus is the "true" vine because of his relationship to God. The true vine is possible because of the vinedresser who gives life and sustains it.

The vinedresser removes non–fruit-bearing branches. The Greek verb translated "remove" (*kathairo*) is used to denote both pruning and cleansing. The cleansing here refers to the issues of ritual uncleanness and cleanness (see Lev. 12 and Num. 19:11). Jesus transforms the association: his words have already cleansed the disciples. Faithfulness is not determined by outward or elaborate rituals; it is determined by one's relationship with God through Jesus.

As the "true vine," Jesus determines the community; who he is determines who the community is. Those who abide in Jesus bear much fruit. This means that believers do the works of Jesus as Jesus does the works of "the Father." There is no harvest or yield if the branches do not issue from the vine.

Those who do not abide in Jesus are like useless branches and are fit only for the fire. The branches that do not yield fruit are the ones in the community who profess faith but do not respond through acts of love. This does not mean that one can *earn* salvation; rather, those who see and hear Jesus are moved to respond to the gift of salvation through their own acts of love. Those who abide in Jesus are rewarded: their prayers will be answered. God always heard the prayers of Jesus and will hear the prayers of the believers. The community is assured of God's presence and care. The evidence of their understanding is seen in their discipleship, the doing of Jesus' work.

The disciples' union with Jesus and God makes for a full joy, just as a well-pruned vine makes for a plentiful harvest.

This union is grounded in the belief that Jesus is God's self-expression. Jesus willingly lays his life down for his friends—evidence of an intimacy much deeper than "friend" conveys. Jesus has given himself fully to his believers; he has harbored no secrets—he has poured himself out to them and for them. Thus, even though they made a decision to believe and follow Jesus, they could do so only in the context of having been chosen already by God and Jesus. God seeks us—all of us—and sent Jesus to fulfill that mission. We can choose to follow or not, but God makes the possibility of choice a reality.

Because God has made choice possible, we have the responsibility to respond. If we choose to follow Jesus, there is a cost: we are appointed to do the works of Jesus and to love one another. The command to love is continued from the foot-washing ceremony and permeates the Gospel. The community has the power of prayer as a leaning-post for their ministries. The community ought to be strengthened by the knowledge that God has provided a means by which they can do the works of God, "the Father."

Thus, Jesus takes the common everyday image of the vine and transforms it into a symbol of community, mission, and love. The community that Jesus forms through his birth and death is characterized by interdependence, mutual respect, and his ongoing presence. The power that Jesus manifests is from God, with whom he is connected. The power we would claim as followers of Christ must come from Jesus. We can have this power *only* if we are connected to Jesus!

MEDITATION

I come from a long line of women and men who have green thumbs. My paternal great-grandmother could bring even the driest, most shriveled plant back to life. Her front porch in Demopolis, Alabama, was a dense garden of plants, vines, and flowers. She planted flowers in old Mason jars, in old buckets, and in old truck tires. She hung vines from the rafters and along the porch railings. Her yard was an incredible array of colors and fragrances.

She passed her green thumb along to her daughter. My grandmother continued her mother's legacy. Her house was overrun with beautiful plants and flowers. She tended them with care, and they flourished. She then passed her green thumb on to my father. Each spring, he turned a small patch of dry dirt in our Chicago backyard into a bounty of strawberries, tomatoes, bell peppers, and beans.

The spring before he died, my father lamented that he was unable to plant his vegetable garden. I volunteered to help him, but he needed to show me how to plant a garden. On a sunny but cool day in late May 1984, we worked in the backyard. He showed me how to turn the dirt, remove rocks and debris, how to work fertilizer into the soil. He showed me how to make mounds and how to drop the seeds into the soil. He showed me how to cover the lifeless, dry seeds and how to water the mounds gently. It was a labor of love and one of the last things my father and I shared. His garden had become *our* garden.

Three weeks later, my father died. After his funeral, I went to sit by our garden. To my surprise, what had been bare mounds the week before now anchored small green shoots! The lifeless, dry seeds were growing; in the face of death, new life emerged.

A year later, my mother wanted to plant rose bushes in the backyard to commemorate the anniversary of my father's death. She and I went to the nursery and chose four small plants. In early June 1985, we planted the bushes. We had been warned by the nursery owner that the plants we chose would not bloom until the following year. The important thing was to plant the roses.

Four weeks later, my mother died. After her funeral, I again went to sit in the backyard, where pleasant memories of my father and mother comforted me. To my amazement, one plant held a perfect pink rose blossom! In the midst of the ugliness of death, new life burst forth!

My siblings and I have since sold my parents' home. No longer can I sit in the backyard that was so precious. I now maintain a garden in my own backyard as a way of staying connected to my parents. Each year I prepare the soil and plant vegetables. Each year I prune and tend to my rose bushes. Each spring I am reminded of the legacy of my parents: an appreciation for nature and beauty; a rootedness in the soil and all that it yields; a life shaped by rural and urban realities. Each spring I am reminded of God's promise of abundant life and God's abiding presence!

It is right and proper that the church celebrates Lent in the spring of the year. This is the time when all that seems dead is resurrected, all that has lain dormant produces new life. This is the time when we are reminded of Jesus' sacrifice and God's promises.

We have spent eight weeks together renewing our connection with God through the lessons and works of Jesus Christ. I hope these studies have awakened some dormant part of your spirituality. I hope you have a sense of my faith journey and my excitement about this adventure. I hope you have been able to reflect on and share your own faith journey with others. I hope you will continue to study; such discipline enriches the journey. And I hope you will engage other spiritual disciplines; such efforts enhance the journey.

Thank you for allowing me to companion with you these past weeks. We now look ahead and see a hill in the distance. We know that our trek leads to Calvary and a cruel, unavoidable crucifixion. But this time, as we gaze at the hill, things are different. We know that the cross is not the final answer. We know that the tragedy of Good Friday cannot keep the joy of Easter Sunday at bay. Not even a tomb can keep Jesus from doing God's work. To God be the glory—Jesus lives!

QUESTIONS FOR REFLECTION

1. Train and plane tickets are perforated pieces of paper. The ticket agents separate the tickets; they keep a part and return a part to us to keep as a receipt. The tickets always clearly state "Void if detached." What does this say about our relationship to Jesus? Explain.

2. The first time I planted cucumbers, I overplanted. One day there were small green plants. Then, almost overnight, my backyard was overrun with trailing, clinging vines, huge green leaves, and bright yellow flowers. They were everywhere! I tried to cut the plants back, but it was too late. I did not even know where to begin—it was just too much! I spent the summer collecting cucumber recipes and giving the fruits away. No one visited my home without taking big bags filled with cucumbers; people stopped coming over! The next year, I paid more attention and pruned my cucumber plants. The harvest was just enough for my friends and me. The work of pruning was time-consuming, but the effort was worth it.

   How is your congregation like a cucumber patch?

   What are the tasks your congregation needs to perform if it is to live as branches of the "true vine"?

   What pruning needs to happen in your life so you yield a fruitful harvest?

   What pruning needs to happen in your congregation?

3. What are the implications of the vine image for church leadership? Explain.

CLOSING PRAYER

Eternal God, you are wonderful! You have seen our needs and satisfied them. We thank you for the perfect gift of Jesus, who makes all things new. Stay with us, O God, until we are safely in your presence for all time. We pray in the blessed name of Jesus, even as we march with him to Calvary. We live in expectation of your promise to raise him up again. We rest in the assurance that you will raise us up to new life. In Jesus' name we pray. Amen.

SUGGESTIONS FOR USING *BREAD OF LIFE* IN TEACHING AND PREACHING

THIS SECTION IS for Bible study leaders. Below are suggestions for using this book in a group setting. This book is designed as an eight-week study, one session for the introduction and one each for the seven Bible lessons. The ideal length of time for each session is one-and-a-half to two hours; feel free, however, to make adjustments that work for your group. Each session might include an opening prayer, the reading of the biblical text, reflection on the story, and a closing prayer. The leader should read the material in the first session before the group meets.

For individuals using this resource, you are encouraged to follow the same pattern with some adjustments. You may want to keep a journal or diary to record your thoughts, feelings, and questions. The last section, "Resources for Further Study," lists some books that will give more information about the texts than this resource can provide. Feel free to include other materials that you find enlightening and inspirational. In addition to recording your thoughts, you may want to include your prayer concerns that arise during this period of Lent and you may want to write out your prayers. Your journal will be a reflection of where you are at the beginning of this study and a sign of where you are at the end of it. Your journey is important; you may want to review your thoughts next year as part of your Lenten reflection time or share your journal with another person.

SESSION 1: THE INTRODUCTION

The first meeting sets the tone for the rest of the study period. It is important that participants get to know each other. First, *open with prayer*—this can be a simple request for God to help the group in its study and reflection. The leader should *introduce the course* and make sure that each participant has a Bible and a copy of this book. Participants should use any Bible with which they feel comfortable. *Bread of Life* is based on the New Revised Standard Version, but other translations are acceptable. In fact, using different translations will provide a broader scope of how the biblical texts have been interpreted and understood. Emphasize that this course is a time of study—participants should have a Bible in which they can highlight, writer and jot notes. The same is true for the handling of this book—participants should feel free to write in the margins as much as they want.

After prayer and a brief overview of the course, the leader should *build community* within the group. Any exercise for breaking the ice is acceptable; it may be a simple task of having each person give his or her name and the reason for taking this course. If participants already know one another well, another tactic might be to have them answer an incomplete sentence such as "For me, Jesus is_____." The aim of community building is to introduce members to one another so that they have some sense of what brings persons to this time of study and reflection.

The leader might want to have the group *establish some ground rules for group life.* These might be listed on newsprint and brought to each session. Some suggestions include:

- The group will respect confidentiality.
- Everyone is expected to be fully engaged, even if persons choose to remain silent.
- No one person will dominate the conversation.

- Disagreements will be permitted, but shouting, name calling, and so on will not.
- The group will start and end sessions within the time frame upon which they have agreed.
- Everyone will come prepared; this means doing homework as assigned!

Let the group decide what the ground rules will be. The list can be shorter or longer than the one above.

The next step is to have participants *read the introductory material in session 1.* If time is short, have the group pay special attention to the section "Who Is 'I Am'?" The leader should answer any questions the group may have about this section.

The last suggestion for the first meeting is to *assign the reading of "Session 2: The Bread of Life"* for the next meeting. The leader should lead the group in *reciting the closing prayer in unison.* After the first meeting, participants will have had the opportunity to read and reflect on the assigned sections prior to the meeting. Sessions 2 through 8, then, will be more participatory and the work of the leader will be easier.

SESSIONS 2–8: THE BIBLE STUDIES

The Bible study sessions should follow the same pattern; feel free to make adjustments that make sense for your group. Feel free, also, to include any other materials that will help in the discussion and reflection. These supplementary materials may include hymns and songs, art, music, or excerpts from other literature. The pattern for sessions 2 through 8 might look like the following:

- *Opening prayer is led by the leader or a volunteer from the group*; the group may decide to select persons in advance to pray. The prayer should ask for God's guidance and inspiration as well as openness to the lesson. The one who prays should use his or her own words. This time might also include a hymn, song, poetry, or short biblical readings.

- *The assigned scripture is read aloud.* One person or a number of persons may do the reading. Although persons will have read the text as homework, reading together breaks the ice and puts everyone on the same level.

- *Discuss the overview.* The leader should ask if the lesson is clear and persons should feel free to ask questions and share their understandings of the text and lesson (10–15 minutes).

- *Discuss the meditation.* For another fifteen or twenty minutes, participants should give their reactions to the ideas highlighted in this section. They may agree, disagree, or seek fuller understanding.

- *Discuss the reflection questions.* This is a time for persons to wrestle with the text and its interpretations. The questions are designed to challenge persons and provide opportunities for them to express their feelings, beliefs, and doubts. The questions are open-ended—there are no right or wrong answers. Do not despair if the group does not get through all the questions; the point is to get them talking about matters of faith and everyday life. If after the first couple of sessions the group does not get through most of the questions, the leader may want to assign one or two questions as a focus.

- *Remind participants of the next meeting's assignment* about ten minutes before the end of the session.

- *Ask if there are special prayer concerns.* If so, pray for the concerns and have the group pray the closing prayer together. It is important for persons to have an opportunity to share their joys and concerns in this setting; they have formed a community, and prayer is as important as study and reflection. This time might also include a hymn, song, poem, or short biblical reading, whatever seems appropriate and meaningful for the group.

At the last session, the closing should be an extended time of celebration—of the presence of the living Christ in your midst, of the community you have formed, of the deepening of faith and understanding through study and reflection together. The group may want to engage in a ritual that celebrates the completion of the course, perhaps awarding ribbons, crosses, certificates, or anything else that symbolizes the act of faith that has occurred over the eight weeks of Lent. These weeks have been a time of prayer, study, reflection, and sharing. This is quite an accomplishment!

Those who are teachers and preachers in the church are challenged to include these passages from John in your ministry. It is hoped that the meditations and reflection questions stimulate creativity for your ministries. For instance, many of the lessons can serve as theological springboards to mission efforts in the community that surrounds the church. Also, you might be stirred to use texts in ways other than the traditional ways; for instance, the meditation "Home" in session 7 may serve as a basis for understanding or establishing a new grief ministry in the church. The reflection questions may serve as the basis for object lessons for youth and adults. The possibilities are endless, and you are encouraged to let your creativity have free reign.

I have not tried to write the definitive commentary on the "I Am" sayings of Jesus in the Gospel of John. I have hoped to prime the pump of your spirituality and biblical understanding of these texts. I have hoped that in sharing my story and perceptions, you will be moved to do the same. I have hoped that this resource will help you make connections between your faith and your life. If I have done even a portion of these aims, I claim success. I pray that as you risk embarking on this journey, our God and Savior will richly reward you with peace, love, community, and hope!

RESOURCES FOR
FURTHER STUDY

Barclay, William. *The Gospel of John*, vols. 1 and 2. Philadelphia: Westminster Press, 1975.

Brown, Raymond E. *The Gospel According to John.* New York: Doubleday, 1970.

Mays, James L., ed. *Harper's Bible Commentary.* San Francisco: Harper & Row, 1988.

O'Day, Gail R. "John." In *The New Interpreter's Bible*, ed. Leander E. Keck, 9:491–866. Nashville: Abingdon, 1995.

Sloyan, Gerard S. *John: Interpretation Series.* Atlanta: John Knox Press, 1988.